LIFE'S TOO SHORT

10/6

Life's Too Short

Helen Rollason with John Caunt

CORONET BOOKS

Hodder & Stoughton

Eleanor Oldroyd's tribute is reproduced
by kind permission of *The Sunday Times*

Copyright © 2000 by Helen Rollason

The right of Helen Rollason to be indentified as the
Author of the Work has been asserted by her in accordance
with the Copyright, Designs and Patents Act 1988.

First published in Great Britain in 2000
by Hodder and Stoughton
First published in paperback in 2001
by Hodder and Stoughton
A division of Hodder Headline

A Coronet Paperback

10 9 8 7 6 5 4 3 2 1

A CIP catalogue record for this title
is available from the British Library.

ISBN 0 340 76773 1

Printed and bound in Great Britain by
Clays Ltd, St Ives plc

Hodder and Stoughton
A division of Hodder Headline
338 Euston Road
London NW1 3BH

Contents

Foreword

by Desmond Lynam

I FIRST became aware of Helen during the 1988 Seoul Olympics. She was then working as a reporter for ITV who were covering those Games in competition with the BBC. Helen seemed to be everywhere, probing, reporting and asking the right questions with care and flair. Post-Games the BBC snapped her up. We became colleagues and would bump into each other from time to time. I loved her smile. We were always working on different programmes though and I even missed being with her at Wimbledon in 1990 because I was presenting the football World Cup that summer.

We talked about her tennis broadcasting afterwards because she thought it had not gone too well. It had actually been better than she feared, but I had been able to console her somewhat because I had made an almighty bloomer myself on a football broadcast from Naples. I told her that I was going to take a deep breath and move on and suggested that she should do precisely the same. She certainly did.

Helen became a highly accomplished broadcaster, her sympathetic and understanding nature making her a most appropriate presenter for the Paralympics and other disabled sport in particular. And of course, not only was she the first woman to present *Grandstand* but, for several years, she had her own Friday sports show on the BBC, plus her regular sports news slots.

When she became ill, she did not hide. On the contrary, her resolution to continue as normal wherever possible was hugely courageous, despite what she said, and gave strength and hope to so many in a similar situation. We began to lunch together occasionally. Her condition ruled out alcohol and I would join Helen on the sparkling water, on which we would get high as kites, gossiping and giggling like adolescents.

We would speak on the telephone from time to time when she would be more concerned about my well-being than her own.

A few months ago, along with John Motson the football commentator and a few other friends, I joined that strange band of people with little judgement and became a racehorse owner. Shortly afterwards I had a conversation with Britain's most famous racing trainer, Jenny Pitman. 'Horses,' she said, 'should be put on the National Health. You should see the good they do for people who are in low spirits or suffering from ill-health when they come to our yard.'

Prompted by this, our syndicate decided to invite Helen to join us. She had been asking about the horse anyway. Helen agreed to be an owner/mascot. We spent a fabulous day at Jim Old's stable in Wiltshire when it was clearly love at first sight for both Helen and Out of the Deep. Afterwards at a pub lunch, Helen looked terrific and was, as I put it to her, 'eating for England', a remark made while she was taking a mouthful, which had her crying with laughter.

That day will be my lasting memory of Helen. What a lady. And what an example she gave to all, of how we should hope to behave when we find ourselves under fire.

Desmond Lynam

Preface

IN the autumn of 1998, just before the QED programme *Hope for Helen* was broadcast, it was suggested to me that I might like to write an autobiography. I didn't fall over myself with enthusiasm. The idea seemed a little pretentious and I wasn't sure I wanted to put my story into print. An article here and there, a TV programme, these I can handle, but a book about my life? No, I don't think that's for me.

There is nothing particularly remarkable about me. I am a forty-three-year-old sports presenter who lives in a comfortable suburban road in commuter-belt Essex with my teenaged daughter and small black cat. Over the past twenty-two months my life has been turned upside down by serious illness. Nothing unusual here either. Many thousands every year are in the same boat. I'm in the public eye, but so what? My circumstances have already received heavy media coverage. What more is there to tell?

So, why did my views change? Change they did, as you've already astutely observed by the fact that you are holding the finished product in your hand.

The first factor was the response I received to the pro-gramme: literally thousands of letters from people I have never met, letters that continue to arrive. People telling stories of hope and courage, people who write about the way the programme has helped them to deal with challenges of all kinds, people who offer their thoughts and prayers, people proffering cancer cures and reliefs. I have been truly overwhelmed and humbled by the response.

Secondly, I reflected on how lucky I have been with the family, friends and colleagues I have around me, and how important they have been in the fight against my illness. I came to realise that the story, the one I want to tell, is as much about them as it is about me.

Several times in recent months there have been flattering references in the media to my fighting spirit. I'm not sure how justified they are, but I know that whatever perseverance I possess is owed in large measure to the example of courage and determination shown by some of the exceptional people I have met in my life and work.

This book then – autobiography still sounds rather grand – is about my life since August 1997. But it's also about the kaleidoscope of previous encounters and experiences that shapes the way we deal with things.

If, in places, I refuse to dwell for long on the darkest moments, you must forgive me. Not only does memory filter out the blackest days as part of the process of healing, but also, for me, a major part of living this crazy incomprehensible life is about seeing the light and the humour in difficult times. Life's just too short to be squandered on negativity.

When you are told you have cancer, you're starting on a journey with the disease. It is not the end of your life, but the start of trying to lead a different life. There's no reason why you can't get out of bed, get through the chemo and have a good day. You've got to try to enjoy each day, and not to think, 'Oh my God! I've got cancer. I can't do anything.' Ultimately you may not survive it. But I passionately believe that your chances of doing so, and the quality of life for you and those around you, are immeasurably enhanced by your attitude towards the disease. You must try to beat it, control it, and do your best to make sure it's not going to get to you, yet.

To a large extent the period since August 1997 has been a voyage of discovery. In the course of it I have been privileged to meet some truly amazing people. I have explored the gamut of therapies from the seriously traditional to the outright cranky. I have re-visited and drawn upon some of the most formative experiences and encounters in my life. I have discovered new resources within myself and those around me. I have experienced the deepest lows and the greatest highs and, more than ever before, I have learned to treasure life.

Helen Rollason
May 1999

1

August 1997

S UNDAY 10th August 1997. I was down to present the sports roundup on the main evening news bulletin and a Breakfast slot the following day. It had been an eventful day in British sport. Gear trouble two laps from home had denied Damon Hill a win in the Hungarian Grand Prix. At the World Athletics Championships in Athens, Britain's men's relay teams had won silver in the 4 × 400 and bronze in the 4 × 100. Australia had won the Fifth Test at Trent Bridge and with it the Ashes, and Manchester United had beaten Spurs 2:0. All nail-biting stuff, but I was feeling particularly under the weather, and having difficulty maintaining my usual enthusiasm. I struggled through the evening session and left Television Centre with some relief around 11 p.m. Presenting a Breakfast session means a four o'clock start, so there was no point in heading off home. On days like this it's a case of checking into a hotel and snatching a few hours sleep.

When you're feeling ill, hotel rooms lose the little charm they may have had, and I was not a happy bunny as I crawled into bed. Almost immediately, I began to experience the most intense pain. Really frightening pain. I called the hotel reception and asked if they could get me a doctor. 'Yes we can,' explained the receptionist. 'But it will cost you £50. You see they have to come out on mopeds.' Now there's an image. Even in my sorry condition I was tickled by the idea of a fleet of moped-riding doctors, buzzing around the streets of central London. If I hadn't felt quite so terrible I might have considered asking the receptionist whether she could get me one on a bicycle for £25.

I'm not a cheapskate but fifty quid seemed a bit over the top, so I decided to grit my teeth and hope the pain would go away. It didn't. Sleep was impossible, and by the time I was due to get up for work, I was barely capable of turning on the television, let alone appearing on it. There was nothing for it but to phone the Breakfast studio and tell them I was unable to make it. No big deal you may think, but I have always hated succumbing to illness and letting people down. There is something stubborn and irrational in me which sees illness – my own not others – as an acknowledgement of defeat, giving in to weakness.

The editor of the day was immediately understanding. He told me not to worry, and arranged for a BBC driver to pick me up from the hotel and take me back to my own car. Somehow I managed to drive myself home.

For a couple of years I had suffered a series of inexplicable health problems, some niggling, others more serious. I had a particularly troublesome time when I was covering the Olympics in July 1996. On the plane to Atlanta I felt nauseous and exhausted. Not a good start. And my general state of health was not helped by the accommodation. I've stayed in some pretty crummy places, but this one would have made Bates Motel seem welcoming. Unfortunately, the BBC were desperate, having been let down badly over a decent hotel in the area. There's a common belief that television presenters spend their overseas assignments in five-star luxury. It's not true, honest!

If you have ever visited the southern states of the USA in summer, you will have no trouble identifying the most essential ingredient of a comfortable and relaxing stay. That's right, air conditioning. Well, my room had air conditioning and it worked. Unfortunately, it sounded like a motor bike and created such a foul smell that I couldn't bear to turn it on. Consequently, I spent stifling, fitful nights vainly trying to capture precious sleep. Hey, perhaps it *was* Bates Motel. Trust old Norman to hide a body in the air conditioning unit.

Working hours at a major sporting event like the Olympics would make a Brussels bureaucrat blanch. An eighteen-hour day is not unusual – incredibly early starts to catch sportsmen and women before their day's preparation begins, morning interviews, afternoon live coverage, evening roundups, preparation of British breakfast-time transmissions – day after day. Now I love hard work and have never had a problem with long hours. I adore the Olympics, but I was finding it very hard going. I could scarcely eat without being ill and suffered severe feverish headaches and constant fatigue.

At the end of the Olympics I had a few days before I was due back in Atlanta to present the Paralympics – just long enough to rush home and spend a few days in Cornwall with my daughter Nikki. In my dash to the West Country I crashed

3

the car – jabbering on the phone, I'm ashamed to admit. I didn't notice until it was too late that the car in front had stopped.

Back in Atlanta, the physical problems recurred. But it was great to have the opportunity to be at the Paralympics again and a real privilege to present them. I have the utmost admiration and respect for the achievements of the paralympian athletes. Not only do they triumph over disability, but at these Paralympics they also had to put up with organisation and accommodation way below that offered to the athletes at the main Olympics.

I attributed my health problems in Atlanta to a combination of heat, humidity and long working hours. But it became clear that there was more to it than this. In midsummer southern USA it was easy enough to blame the climate, but when the same symptoms started to show up in bleak old Essex, that explanation began to look pretty thin.

In the following twelve months I was repeatedly unwell, and was back and forth to the doctor and the hospital for health checks, specialist consultations and tests. Still the problems persisted and neither I nor the doctors had any idea what was wrong. Various possibilities were discussed: Crohn's disease, food allergy, Celiac disease, stomach ulcers. Something was seriously wrong, I sensed it. I was working hard, but not appreciably more than normal, and I was not conscious of any undue stress. My normally reliable body was just not matching up to my expectations of it. I found myself having to take some form of painkiller most days.

It's interesting just how long an outdated self-definition can persist. I am a fit and healthy person. That's what I've always been. That's what the people around me see me as. This pain I'm feeling doesn't fit with that definition.

What do you do in circumstances like these? Well, if you're like I was, you stupidly push it to the back of your mind and get on with your life and work as best you can. I even started to regard the aches and pains as normality. Doesn't everyone include paracetamol as part of their daily diet?

In the summer of '97 I started to get periodic bouts of fever. They occurred about once a fortnight and seemed to be at times when I had been working particularly hard. Typical was one which occurred in July when Nikki and I were due to leave for a surfing break in Cornwall with friends. The night before we left I was really rough, but we both needed the holiday. Staying home was not an option. I was quite distressed but consoled myself in the belief that, yet again, the problem would go away. It did, although the friends we joined were staggered by my condition when we arrived – breathless, yellow and so tired. After a couple of days I started to get my strength back and began to enjoy myself. In fact, I had a fabulous time cycling, walking, surfing. I even learned to stand on a surfboard, although not for long enough to sing the first two bars of 'Surfing USA'. At forty-one I might have left it just a trifle too late for a career as a globetrotting professional surfer.

Monday 11th August, and here I was just a few weeks later, back in the doctor's surgery after my frightening night in the London hotel. My doctor took a blood test and I wondered whether I could be suffering from ME. When you don't know what you've got, you might as well introduce a bit of variety into your speculation. This time the problems didn't disappear after a few days. I was unable to do anything serious in the way of work throughout that or the following week. On Friday Nikki left for a holiday in France with friends and I chugged along, hoping to throw off this latest bodily rebellion.

The following Wednesday, I went for a second blood test, then on to the women's England v South Africa one-day match at Lord's which I was due to present for the BBC. I was so breathless going up the stairs to the box, that I had to stop for a rest half way. During the game I was sitting next to John Major and I can recall feeling pretty miserable. I can't blame him for that. There you go, John! That must be one of the few things you haven't been blamed for in the last decade.

The crowd at Lord's was small, which was a great shame. Women's cricket can be absorbing. On that day, England beat South Africa by seven wickets. In 1993 they won the World Cup and were semi-finalists in 1997. In the last few years, other countries, particularly Australia and New Zealand, have caught up and overtaken us, but it is still enjoyable. John Major, incidentally, has been a supporter of the women's game for a number of years. As I write, the first female playing members are being admitted to the MCC. Coming on top of last year's vote which opened the way to women membership, that's progress indeed. It has only taken 211 years to achieve.

Two days later Dr Hildebrand called about the blood test. 'You're critically anaemic. We can't believe you are standing up. We need you to get to hospital right away for some further tests.' Some builders had just arrived at my house to carry out a loft conversion. 'I've got to go to hospital today, guys. I'll just leave you to it. See you tomorrow.' Six weeks later, when I finally returned, they were still there and had almost finished their tea break. Only joking, lads!

Only on the Bank Holiday Monday after two blood transfusions was I well enough for the tests. Tests! What an innocuous word. For anybody who hasn't been through the ritual, the word evokes images of white coats and intricate measurements. The reality is as much a test of your dignity as your medical condition. Short of calling in Dyno-rod, every conceivable means of probing and examining my inner workings seemed to be employed. I remember being shocked and scared. It didn't take a genius to conclude that this level of activity would not be happening on a Bank Holiday unless something pretty serious was afoot.

I had only told one or two people that I was going into hospital and hadn't thought to ask a friend to accompany me on the day of the tests. Hartswood Hospital is only three miles from my home, but it might have been three hundred. I felt very alone and frightened. Thank goodness for a lovely nurse, Kelly, who was with me throughout the day.

Towards the end of the day, Dr Peter Willoughby had the unenviable task of telling me the outcome. Cancer of the colon with secondaries, scale as yet unknown, in the liver.

It wasn't a total surprise. I guess that cancer had been one of the possibilities lurking in my mind for some time, but you don't want to bring it to the forefront of your attention. Like all the really scary things in life, it's best considered at the end of a line of less dramatic and more likely explanations.

No, it wasn't a surprise, but that didn't lessen the shock.

How do you deal with that sort of shock? Being told on a

Bank Holiday Monday afternoon that your life may be coming to an abrupt end. There's no training for it, no correct way to behave. I remember the emotional whirlpool. Sorry about the cliché, but that is how it was: stifling fear, anger, loss of control, intense anxiety for the future, myself, my friends and family – particularly my loving teenaged daughter. Everything changes at that moment. A few minutes before you are deeply worried, hoping you're wrong, not wanting to consider the worst. Then, suddenly, you're struggling to get to grips with this thing you are being told, this new frightening reality in your life.

Looking back on it, I think my television training kicked in at that point. Golden rules: don't show emotion on camera, stay calm in a crisis. Things can, and quite often do, go pear-shaped in the middle of a live broadcast. You're getting all sorts of signals and noises in your ear, but you have to retain your cool and make it through to the end. So it was with this, the most frightening news of my life. While my brain ran around in absolute terror, my poor mouth was on automatic pilot, dealing with the situation as best it could. What came out was calm and composed, but ridiculously mundane and inadequate. 'OK, OK, OK. What now?' I fully appreciated the gravity of what I was being told, but my response was more akin to somebody being told that their central heating boiler needed replacing.

Dr Willoughby finally had to tell me to stop saying OK. 'It's not OK.'

Of course, shock hits you in unexpected ways. You may be able to comprehend bad news rationally, but need time to adjust to it emotionally. I didn't cry, couldn't cry as Dr Willoughby told me the scale of the problem. I cried plenty in the days that followed.

Dr Willoughby brought in a colleague, a surgeon, Mr Ribeiro, and between them they outlined the situation and what they proposed to do about it. They explained to me that the tumours in the liver were a much greater worry than the one in the colon. I could see that they were shocked by the extent to which the cancer had already spread. The colon was something which should be operable, but depending on the scale of the secondary tumours it might already be too late for surgical intervention on the liver. They proposed to operate on the colon within the following couple of days and to assess damage to the liver at the same time.

The competence of doctors tends to be judged in terms of technical skills and knowledge. But when it comes to presenting the diagnosis of a life-threatening disease, I can't think of any job in which communication and people skills play a more important part. Doctors have to make the diagnosis understandable, help the person to absorb the information, and manage denial or extremes of emotion. They need to be prepared for the varied ways in which people will react to shock, and be sensitive to personality and the individual perceptions, myths, experiences and horror stories which make one person react differently from another. Perhaps the most difficult challenge of all is to be open and honest while not destroying hope. The old-fashioned stereotype of a consultant – you know the sort James Robertson Justice used to play – didn't bother about people's feelings. Patients were just receptacles for interesting symptoms. I wonder whether there are consultants like that still around? I'm pleased that I've not come across any.

When it had all been said, and the doctors left, I felt more alone than I think at any time in my life. Certainly friends turned up almost immediately and the nurses were wonderfully caring and considerate. But it was a time when no caring professional can substitute for a really trusted close relative or best friend. My sister Ali who, after Nikki, is the relative I have the closest relationship with, was on an expedition in South America. Nikki was in France with a good friend. Others who might have helped were miles away and unaware. That's when I did manage to cry.

The business of having to tell others, while coming to terms with it myself, was not easy. I was due in at work the day after my cancer was diagnosed and so I needed to tell them. I phoned BBC Breakfast Sport on the Tuesday morning. Nick Dickson and Rob Bonnet, two colleagues I'm very fond of, were there. Nick picked up the phone and I said, 'I'm sorry to tell you this but I've got cancer. I don't know when I'll be back.' I could just sense the shock at the other end of the line. I felt guilty for doing that to them, felt somehow I needed to apologise.

A few minutes after my conversation with Nick and Rob, Andrew Thompson, the Head of Breakfast, phoned me. It was slightly easier for me this time, since I didn't have to break the news. He suggested the need to inform people within the BBC why I wasn't there. I agreed with a bit of reluctance. Of course, it didn't stay internal news for long. Within hours the press had hold of it. There were press at the hospital, press phoning other colleagues and friends of mine who at that stage didn't know.

By the following day it was all over the newspapers. Some of my best friends learned of my illness while on holiday, reading a newspaper by the pool – not the ideal way to break the news. Most of them were absolutely wonderful about it, but just one or two were really cross they found out that way. Makes me wonder what they would have expected me to do. Was I supposed to ring round and say, 'Hello, I've got cancer'?

The media interest was both a nuisance and a help. The downside was the inevitable intrusion. Neighbours told me later that there were photographers camped out on my lawn the morning after the announcement. My mother and my friends were pestered. The hospital had to start screening telephone calls.

On the plus side, the actual coverage was overwhelmingly positive, and arising from it I received a huge number of letters. I never realised that so many people even knew who I was, let alone cared. Letters were arriving by the sackful and, although I was not able to deal with them at the time, it was an immense source of strength to think that so many people felt moved enough to write. Later, when I was well enough to read them properly, they were really important to me as I worked to get my life back together. Masses of flowers were delivered to the hospital. It's a tiny hospital and they were just everywhere.

Newspapers repeatedly emphasised my fighting qualities – 'If anyone can beat it, she can.' Very flattering in normal circumstances, but when I was at my most vulnerable it felt like an added responsibility. It was like, 'If I don't beat this, it will be my fault for not trying hard enough.'

My operation was scheduled for Wednesday, two days after the diagnosis. The doctors thought it was important that my daughter was called back to England. She arrived just before I went into the operation. I can see her stricken sad face as she came through the door of my room. My friends, with whom she had been on holiday, had understandably tried to spare her the seriousness of the situation. But an entire family doesn't abandon a foreign holiday in mid-term and return home over a run-of-the-mill illness. She knew it was serious. Not easy for a fourteen-year-old. She had left what she thought was a reasonably healthy mother, and returned less than two weeks later to find her with tubes hanging out of every orifice. The sight of her made me want to cry, but she also managed to make me laugh. 'Other people's mums get appendicitis or need hysterectomies. You have to go one better don't you, and get the very worst thing you could possibly have.'

Bernie Ribeiro, the surgeon, is a delightful man. I have to admit that I had not given a lot of thought to surgeons before, but if somebody is going to cut you open, he's the sort of person you would want to do it. I would describe him as the Des Lynam of surgery – could charm for England. He has even got the moustache.

The operation to remove the tumour on the colon was initially successful, but an examination of the liver confirmed that it was full of secondary tumours and that there was nothing surgically that could be done at this stage. The prognosis was extremely bleak. I was very weak after the operation and in a great deal of pain. My memory has filtered out some of the awfulness of it, but friends who spent a lot of time with me

12

in those critical days, remember me crying from the pain and begging for some respite from it.

In the middle of all this, I had woken on the Sunday after the operation to learn of the death of Princess Diana. It was the only news topic that week, and it seemed so chillingly close to home – the fact that my life was on the line and her life had gone. There were those boys who had lost their mother and I was distraught about Nikki being without me. I'd brought her up alone for seven years and we are very close. But although Diana's death brought home the seriousness of my own situation, at the same time it gave us an emotional focus which was away from me. The whole country was so taken up with the mourning, the flowers and all the images. Suddenly there was somebody else deserving of our attention – 'there are those poor boys and I'm still here.' We cried a lot, and in retrospect that was very therapeutic. It allowed us to release a lot of the emotion associated with my situation, in a way which was not inward-looking or self-pitying.

Within a few days of the operation a problem developed I couldn't eat, and yet I was constantly nauseous. My stomach was being drained every twenty minutes or so and my weight went down below six stone. It emerged that the problem was a twist in the intestine. On 10th September, two weeks after my original operation, I had to undergo a second emergency operation to sort out the obstruction.

After that, I seemed to be going downhill fast and the tumours in the liver kicked in badly. I was being fed intravenously from a large bag through what seemed to be an exceptionally big hole in my neck. This required very special attention to hygiene and safety and, although I was allowed visitors, my room began to resemble an isolation ward.

I was alarmed to discover that my sense of smell had become incredibly sensitive. Any unfamiliar smell made me sick. If a nurse came in with a new perfume on, I knew it before she had got through the door. And I found it absolutely unbearable if a person had smoked, even several hours previously. I had to be sure that everyone was clean and didn't smell of anything. It became a joke among the nurses. I knew everything they had been eating, drinking and doing. I could just smell it. If only I had been able to scuttle around on all fours, there could have been a new career for me sniffing out illegal drugs at Heathrow Airport.

I had been concerned that members of my family should not rush up to Essex to see me as poorly as I was. But when my sister Ali returned from her adventures in South America and was told about my illness, she and my rather frail mother came to the hospital together as quickly as they could. Dr Willoughby was very frank with them about my chances, and they found it pretty hard to deal with. It's at times like these that you want to help and protect your family, but, of course, when you're as ill as I was there's not a lot you can do. I found that difficult. My mum busied herself with the sacks of letters, opening and sorting them for me. It was a practical task that lifted the anxiety a bit, and the letters' contents made a difference to the mood, gave us a sense of so many other people rooting for me.

In truth, my prospects of survival, for even a short time, were very poor. It was clear that after the second operation there was nothing more that could be done surgically at that time and, without some radically different approach, the doctors believed I would just fade away and die. They proposed bringing in an oncologist, but were not hugely optimistic about the prospect of a positive outcome. In my desperately weak condition, chemotherapy itself could kill me.

I, too, was conscious of the need to do something different. I had to take a grip on it mentally. It was as if everything so far had been happening to somebody else. I felt almost like a spectator in my own body, conscious of all that was taking place, but unable to influence it in any way. I recall vividly the night before my first visit from the oncologist, the realisation that if I didn't do something to turn it around myself, I was going to die. And it was very strange, an almost religious experience – and yet I'm not a religious person – I felt some arms around me. I could actually feel the weight of the arms. Mentally the whole thing started to change from that point. It was as if I had gathered up some new resources within myself and was able to say, 'OK, I can do this. I can pick myself up.'

It's easy to rationalise the experience afterwards – the effect of pain-killing drugs maybe, or the product of my weakened state and blitzed emotions. I have read since that similar experiences are not uncommon among people in life-threatening situations. It's easy to understand how something like this can reinforce religious beliefs, and I don't want to knock that explanation. It just doesn't altogether work for me. But more of that later. The fact is that searching for an explanation is not important. I came out of the moment ready to do battle with the cancer, determined not to fade away. That's the bit that matters, isn't it?

Others were just as determined. My friend Dawn, who had become increasingly worried by the lack of action, had even taken all my scans to a specialist liver surgeon in Basingstoke, Mr Myrddin Rees. I was to find out later what a special person he is. Scans in hand, she waited outside his consulting room until he would see her, and then pressed for an opinion on whether there was any chance he could operate immediately. The news was not good, but I so admired her tenacity.

The oncologist brought in by the hospital was Dr Neville Davidson who has proved to be, quite literally, my lifesaver. But we gave him a hard time at that first meeting. My friends Hazel and Dawn had been at the hospital all day, increasingly anxious about my continued decline and determined to see some new approach to my treatment. Dr Davidson arrived quite late in the evening and we subjected him to a grilling about his credentials, me being sick all the time I was trying to talk to him. 'Why should we go with you? How do we know we're not going down a blind alley? What are you going to do? Shouldn't we be going to the Marsden or somewhere like that? Why you?'

He took it in his stride. I now know him to be a man of immense stature and capability. He convinced us that we needed to let him try a certain course of chemotherapy with all its ghastly implications. There were, he pointed out, serious risks to chemotherapy at this time, and he would not consider starting it for another five days to give me a little more chance to recover from the operations. We agreed, there really were no alternatives, and I moved into a new phase of my life. One that is still with me.

2

When You Need Inspiration

THERE is a limit to the amount of determination you can dredge up from your own resources. When things get really shitty you need the example and inspiration of others to help preserve your will to win. Lying in my hospital bed during those first awful weeks following my diagnosis, I needed inspiration like never before. I was fortunate in having plenty to draw upon, and right up at the top of my list were the people I have met through my work with disability sport. More than any other athletes they have represented for me the triumph of human spirit that illuminates the very best of sporting moments. I have returned to these memories repeatedly, and I can't over-emphasise the help they have been to me.

I've been involved with disability sport for a number of years now, and have presented the last two Paralympic Games for the BBC. The 1992 Games in Barcelona were a huge success, a real joy to attend, but it was to the experience of the Atlanta Paralympics in 1996 that my thoughts most often turned.

As you already know, the Atlanta Olympics hadn't been a particularly happy time for me health-wise. It had been a punishing stint and I didn't like Atlanta. The bad organisation, suffocating heat and soulless feel to the place had left me totally drained. There was a matter of days between the Olympics and Paralympics and, as I snatched that brief holiday in Cornwall, I wasn't exactly itching to get back. But in the back of my mind there was a little buzz. No, it wasn't overuse of the mobile phone, but a feeling that this Paralympics was going to be special. The BBC had allocated ten forty-five-minute programmes to the Games, far more than previously. It meant that the story could unfold throughout the ten days of competition. As I got on to the plane, to be greeted by the same crew that had carried me back to England just a few days previously, I knew I was up for it.

Sport for people with disabilities has developed over the last fifty years. The large number of injured service people and civilians in the aftermath of World War Two prompted new approaches to rehabilitation, and at the Spinal Injuries Centre at Stoke Mandeville Hospital, Dr Ludwig Guttman introduced sports for reasons of therapy and meaningful leisure activity. Within a short time a greater element of competition was introduced, and the momentum which led to today's Paralympic Games was established.

Guttman organised the first Stoke Mandeville Games in 1948 to coincide with the Olympic Games in London. It was a purely domestic affair and limited to wheelchair competition, but during the 1950s other groups linked up with the Stoke

Mandeville Centre and the first Olympic-style games for athletes with a disability was organised in Rome in 1960. From
those small beginnings the Games have steadily grown, and
by the Atlanta Games of 1996 there were no fewer than
seventeen sports involving more than 3500 competitors from
120 countries.

The common perception of disabled competition in this
country is of wheelchair athletes, largely as a result of the
London Marathon coverage. In fact, people with all kinds of
disabilities are able to participate in the Paralympics, and the
range has been progressively widened over the years. A rather
complicated classification system aims to ensure that competitors are matched against others with roughly comparable levels
of disability. Medals are awarded in each of the classification
groupings, so that overall many more medals are presented than
would be the case in an event for able-bodied athletes. Some
sports are geared to particular types of disability. Basketball,
for example, is an exclusively wheelchair sport. Other sports,
such as athletics and swimming, cater for a much wider range
of disabilities. There are classification groupings for competitors
with visual impairments, cerebral palsy, amputees and those
in wheelchairs. There are even some sports which have been
specially invented for athletes with one particular disability.

Enough of the technicalities. What about the inspiration?

Well, there are sufficient examples of courage and determination among the paralympians to fill the remainder of this
book – something I clearly can't do unless I plan to change
the title. So, with apologies to everybody I haven't space to
mention, let me focus on two people, both from the British

team, whom I particularly admire, and whose spirit captures everything that the Paralympics is about.

Noel Thatcher is a physiotherapist from Harlow. He was thirty years old at the time of the Atlanta Paralympics and had previously won gold in the 800 metres at Seoul and the 1500 metres at Barcelona in the category for athletes with visual impairment. This time he decided that he would try to emulate the feat of his hero, Emil Zatopek, who won gold in the 5000 metres, 10,000 metres and the marathon at the 1952 Olympic Games. As Noel said when I interviewed him, 'You've got to find some new dream to get you up on those cold winter mornings in Harlow.'

Noel set himself a punishing training regime, including several weeks in early 1996 with the Japanese Olympic Marathon squad. Shortly before the start of the Paralympics he developed a dull pain in his leg which became intense when he put his weight on it – the classic sign of a stress fracture. When he arrived at the British pre-Games training camp he was referred for scans which confirmed the diagnosis. But Noel wasn't going to be beaten. He hadn't come that far to head off home again. He was determined to line up for the start of the 10,000 metres, his first race. He made it, not only to the start line, but to the finish line in the gold medal position with a new world record, and attracted headlines like 'Man With Broken Leg Wins Gold For Britain' in the press next day.

The media interest in him helped to raise the profile of the Games, but it also increased the expectation of him in the 5000 metres. He didn't disappoint. Throughout a race run in torrential rain, he remained at the shoulder of the Lithuanian front runner before storming past him on the final bend to take his second gold.

Not surprisingly, Noel was in such pain the following day that he could hardly walk. His final event, the marathon, was only twenty-four hours away and the team doctor warned that he should not even contemplate running it. The stresses of running twenty-six miles, particularly the pressure of the downhill stretches, could cause his leg to snap without warning. Reluctantly Noel conceded that the marathon was out of the question, but within hours was planning his campaign for Sydney 2000 and the possibility of achieving the treble. Now that's positive thinking.

Tanni Grey is another person who doesn't give up. With four gold medals at the Barcelona Paralympics and victory in the London Marathon, she was already the best known of Britain's women wheelchair athletes. Slim, almost fragile in her wheelchair, Tanni's appearance is deceptive. She is able to combine the power and acceleration needed to win a 100 metres sprint with the tough as boots endurance required for success over twenty-six miles.

Top-level success at both extremes of the distance scale is unheard of in able-bodied athletics. Sprinting and distance running draw upon quite different physical capabilities. For wheelchair athletes the disparity is not quite so great but Tanni's feat is remarkable nonetheless.

Back in the mists of our evolution we were equipped with the capabilities to meet two distinct requirements for speed of movement. The first was the need to run like the clappers to the nearest tree when chased by some larger creature intent on having us for lunch. The second was the ability to track less aggressive animals than ourselves, often over long distances, in order to keep ourselves in bisonburgers and fur coats.

In the case of the sprint to the tree, valuable time would have been wasted if we had relied upon our hearts and lungs supplying extra oxygen to the muscles, so we developed special muscle fibres which are able to utilise their energy stores without oxygen. These produce an immediate burst of speed, but can only keep going for a matter of seconds before they have to hand the baton over to another group of fibres which can chug along for hours using oxygen to metabolise their fuel.

In most of us there is a roughly equal split of these 'fast twitch' and 'slow twitch' fibres, but some lucky souls have very much higher proportions of one or the other, and these are the people who have the capability to become élite sprinters or distance runners. The proportions of muscle fibres are genetically determined, so no matter how hard he trains, Linford Christie isn't going to come in at the head of a marathon field, and Liz McColgan won't be breaking the tape in the 100 metres.

Such was Tanni Grey's success in Barcelona and the intervening years that she came to Atlanta almost as the symbol of British wheelchair athletics. People were expecting her to repeat the victories of four years previously. That was a tall order because the competition, like the weather in Atlanta, was very hot. Her foremost rival was the very talented American teenager Leann Shannon. The two were well clear of the rest of the field in every race from 100 to 800 metres, but the American's superior sprinting power told in the shorter events and Tanni had to content herself with silver in the 100, 200 and 400. She stormed through to take the gold in the 800, but by her demanding standards, one gold medal was a disappointment, which was not helped by failure to get into the medals in the final event of the Games, the marathon.

When I interviewed her after the 400 metres, Tanni was already looking forward to 'interesting' future competition with Leann. She has continued to notch up victories at various distances and has finished first and second in the London Marathon in the last two years.

People who encounter disability sport for the first time are astonished by the standards achieved by disabled athletes. At the highest level they are comparable with the best able-bodied athletes. Take the Nigerian sprinter Adeoye Ajibola as an example. In his career he has run quickly enough to qualify for the Nigerian Olympic team. 'Why didn't they pick him?' you ask. Well, he has only one arm and so falls foul of the rules which state that sprinters must start with both hands on the track. Crazy isn't it? When you take account of the way a runner's arm action contributes to speed and balance, you have to conclude that Adeoye's feat outstrips similar times by two-armed athletes.

Consider also the achievement of Hou Bin from China. He lost a leg in a train accident as a child. He won a gold medal in the high jump at the Paralympics with a jump of 1.92 metres. That's almost 6 foot 4. Many athletes in this competition were using prosthetic limbs, but not Hou Bin. He bounded up to the pole on one leg!

And what about the American sprinter Tony Volpentest.

He achieved his gold medal with a 100 metres time of 11.36 seconds, running on two prosthetic legs! And as if that wasn't enough, you have to note that Tony's arms are not fully formed, and finish just past the elbow, thus denying him some of the counteractive propulsion that comes from the pumping action of the upper limbs.

I often get told that watching disabled competition is to watch sub-standard sport. Nothing makes me more angry than this. The point is completely missed. The competition is the point, not the small time differences which may distinguish disabled performances from able-bodied ones. People who make these comments wouldn't make similar comparisons between a race run at altitude and one at sea level, even though the effects on the athletes – an additional obstacle to be overcome – may be the same.

There's still an unfortunate tendency in our society to regard hard physical activity or challenging work of any sort as some-how undesirable for disabled people. It's an attitude that may be well meaning enough, but it arises from an old-fashioned notion that people with disabilities need to be wrapped in cotton wool and follow gentle activity – the same thinking that decreed basket-making and piano tuning to be the only legitimate occupations for generations of blind people. And for all the hype about improving opportunities for people with disabilities, we still have a very long way to go.

I have felt strongly about this for some time, but since I developed cancer, my indignation has increased, because I have come face to face with some similar attitudes towards myself. For some people my illness means that I shouldn't be working. In their mild disapproval lies the assumption that when something goes awry in your body it's time to shut up shop as far as any demanding activity is concerned. What they don't seem to realise is that challenge and a sense of contribution is an immensely important part of leading a meaningful life.

I passionately believe that all disabled people – whether or not they are able to work, or take part in sport – have a right to fulfil or exceed their potential, a right to concentrate on abilities rather than disabilities and to experience the thrill of overcoming challenge. This is why the Paralympics are so important. They cast aside some of those old myths about disability. They demonstrate to the able-bodied public and to other disabled people that with dedication and self-belief tremendous things are possible.

Not everything about the 1996 Paralympics was positive. In fact, aspects of the organisation were outrageously bad. The Olympics were under the control of the Atlanta Committee for the Olympic Games (ACOG) while the Atlanta Paralympic Organising Committee (APOC) managed the second event. Choosing acronyms that sound like a pair of warring trolls might be an invitation to friction, and certainly there was no sense of co-operating in a single enterprise. The two might have been staging wholly different competitions.

Before the start of the Paralympics the ACOG planned to take down the 197 flags of the world nations around the stadium which would have left the place largely bereft of its unique big-event atmosphere. Surely they could have been persuaded to leave them up for a few more days? No way!

If gold medals had been awarded for petty officialdom, the ACOG would have swept the board. Fortunately, some good old Aussie common sense came to the rescue in the form of the Sidney 2000 organising committee which stepped in, purchased the flags and then donated them back to the Paralympics. What a ridiculous situation!

Accommodation was not without problem either. ACOG had fallen behind in its post-Olympic cleaning schedule, and some paralympian athletes arrived to rooms which appeared to have been previously occupied by followers of Attila the Hun – stained carpets, rubbish and appliances yanked out of walls. Imagine the delight of one British athlete who was confronted with a carpet liberally decorated in dried vomit. Not quite the international celebration of physical endeavour he was expecting from the Games!

There were a number of cases where two wheelchair athletes were allocated shared study bedrooms which would have been a squeeze for a pair of able-bodied people. Accommodation managers appeared to have overlooked the fact that a wheelchair occupies at least four times the space of a standing person and needs additional room for turning. For the unfortunate room-mates every simple task – washing, teeth cleaning, getting dressed – acquired the complexity of a space station docking manoeuvre. In addition, athletes had to contend with late buses, lost luggage and long queues for very indifferent food in the dining rooms. They bore these tribulations with patience, in stark contrast to some of the Olympic prima donnas who could be thrown into ballistic rage by the tiniest inconveniences.

Within the Paralympic movement itself, there were tensions caused by the complex nature of the disability classification system. This is intended to match athletes with roughly similar levels of disability, but it can throw up some strange anomalies. Aimee Mullions, a double amputee long jumper, complained about the fact that she was competing with two prosthetic legs against people who were wrist amputees. 'I don't see how it can be seen as equal,' she said. 'It's like me competing against an arm amputee on the parallel bars at gymnastics.' She had a point. Generally the classification system works well, but there is only so far that you can go with disability subdivisions. Taken to its logical extreme you would end up with some events having just one competitor.

The disability classification issue raises a fundamental point about the purpose of sport which can be overlooked in our quest for medals and championships. At bottom it's about us triumphing over the limitations of our own unique bodies. That's what the Paralympics is all about, but it also lies at the base of all athletic endeavour. Inherited characteristics and environment give some able-bodied athletes distinct advantages over others. Competition between individuals will never be wholly equal.

As a teenager my great athletic interest was in sprinting. At 5 foot 1? You've got to be joking! My little legs had to work at twice the speed of some taller competitors. But I acquitted myself reasonably well and, while I knew that I would never emulate my heroine, Lillian Board, there was great satisfaction to be gained from pushing my body beyond itself. It's that same struggle against the limitations of the body that keeps me going today.

The Atlanta Paralympics were opened by Superman, Christopher Reeve. Just over a year previously the forty-two-year-old film star had been left paralysed from the neck down following an horrific riding accident during a cross-country event in Virginia. The end of the line for any public activity you may think, but not a bit of it. Despite the most limiting of disabilities, he has continued to devote himself to education and charity. He is undoubtedly even more of a Superman than he was before the accident.

I had the privilege of interviewing him in Atlanta – the most memorable interview I have ever done. It was just an astonishing experience. Here was this man, unable to use any of his limbs to even the slightest degree, or even to breathe without the aid of a respirator. He could barely speak, because he had to fit in his speech with the action of the respirator. He was totally reliant on a posse of minders and nurses. He described for me the routines he had to go through just in order to stay alive and the amazing daily performance that accompanied those things we take for granted – washing, dressing, eating and moving about. And in all this there was not a hint of anger or self-pity. The only time that sadness crossed his handsome face was when he spoke about his three-year-old son and how he found it very difficult that he was unable to cuddle him.

Here was a man who had participated competitively in all manner of sports – riding, sailing, tennis, gliding and skiing. He was also an accomplished pianist who loved to compose and play classical music. I cannot begin to imagine the agony of being pitched from all that into a situation of complete immobility. And yet he was able to talk with enthusiasm about the joy of the paralympians achieving medals and how privileged he felt to be able to open the event. At the times when I have been really ill, really down, I have returned to that meeting for strength and inspiration.

Reeve knows the effect of his example on others. Millions, like me, must have been inspired by him. But there is nothing contrived or self-glorifying about him. Well before his accident, he worked on behalf of causes as diverse as child poverty, human rights and environmental issues. There was always far more too him than the amiable hunky Superman image. At the time I interviewed him, he was already busy with appearances and speaking engagements across America in support of disability issues, and he went on later that year to set up the Christopher Reeve Foundation to raise money for spinal cord injury research and grants to improve quality of life for people with disabilities. He became Chairman of the American Paralysis Association and Vice-Chairman of the National Organisation on Disability. He also moved back into film work: narrating a documentary on disabilities, taking roles in two TV movies and directing his first film *In the Gloaming* which received five Emmy nominations. Last year he produced his autobiography – *Still Me*.

All of that was in the future at the time I spoke to him, but I have been interested recently to read comments from his wife Dana about the effect of this work upon him. She said, 'There's such a difference to his outlook, his health, his overall sense of well-being when he's working at what he loves, which is creative work – directing a movie or acting in one. It completely revitalises him and feeds him. His health is at an all time high . . . he sleeps better, he looks better. It's noticeable – it's like being in love.'

Now I can relate to that.

NBC was prepared to cough up $456 million for the privilege of broadcasting the Atlanta Olympics. What do you think they paid to broadcast the Paralympics? That's right – nothing! Even worse, APOC had to pay $1 million to get the Games shown on American television. As a result there were limited funds available to spend on production and only three of the fourteen Paralympic venues had outside broadcast facilities with multiple cameras. The remaining eleven had to be covered with single camera crews. Live coverage was impossible.

At events like this, overseas broadcasters such as the BBC are heavily dependent on the hosts. That can be frustrating, particularly when an event of national significance is receiving only cursory coverage. In spite of the difficulties, we had assembled a really good team with top-flight swimming and athletics commentators, and I had great fun fronting the programmes.

Every morning at eleven we had to feed the programme on the satellite. It had been put together overnight from the previous day's mixture of sport, features, interviews and pieces to camera. At the crack of dawn we would set about the task of frantically scripting and voicing the programme in order to get it out on time. The timing of the satellite link left little margin for error and, as with all television, we hit the occasional technical problem. These are the times when confidence in your colleagues is tested to the limit, but the production team was almost unflappable. With the programme transmitted, there was no time to rest on our laurels, as the round of preview interviews and features needed to be done before getting into the day's sporting action.

After the relative disappointment of the Olympics, with just one gold medal for Britain, our paralympians came up with a hatful. The squad amassed 39 gold, 42 silver and 41 bronze, and finished fourth in the medal table. Most important, however, was the sense of advancement about the Games as a whole. It really was the occasion when the Paralympics came of age. Countries which had previously made little impact started to enter the frame, reflecting growing awareness and facilities for disabled sport. Records tumbled all over the place as a result of better training methods and improved design of prosthetic limbs and wheelchairs. And there was much greater interest in the coverage provided by my fellow commentators and journalists. Returning to the UK after the Paralympics it was wonderful to find that so many of the sportsmen and women had become household names.

A few weeks ago I attended a fund-raising lunch in aid of the British Wheelchair Sports Federation. I was honoured to be there – guests included Prince Charles, Kate Hoey MP, and many top sportspeople – but I found myself wondering why on earth this part of the Paralympic set up has to beg for money. Wouldn't it be great if we could look forward to the day when sport for people with disabilities was not seen as the poor relation and when the media, sponsors and the general public truly viewed paralympians as élite athletes who happen to have disabilities rather than disabled people who happen to be athletes.

3

September 1997 to January 1998

Getting to grips with a cancer diagnosis is a very important stage in dealing with the disease. Among many other
things you have got to understand what you're up against,
find your way through the inevitable emotional upheaval the
diagnosis brings, adjust your lifestyle and develop coping stra-
tegies. In most circumstances there will be a period of weeks
or months following the diagnosis during which these things
can happen, but in my case I was plunged straight from
diagnosis into a desperate fight for life. It was only after the
immediate crisis that I was really able to turn my mind to some
of these issues.

I approached this task as I would research for a piece of
work, reading everything I could on the subject. If you are
going to get worthwhile answers you have to ask the right
questions; and you can only know the right questions by
being fully informed. It's an important principle when you
are preparing to conduct an interview – vital when you are

looking at options for prolonging your life. I wanted to be sure that no possible avenue was left unexplored. At one point I got Dr Willoughby to sit down and write a list of all the alternative treatment possibilities. There were about twenty. Most were ruled out for one reason or another.

At first, my reading was confined to matters of immediate consequence, the things that were currently happening to me. Some of it was rather unsettling. Material I read about chemotherapy – the programme I was just starting – suggested that it didn't work. Not a great confidence booster for a treatment that has been presented as your only hope.

Later, after I left hospital, I explored the disease from every angle – conventional and alternative. I devoured everything there was to read – autobiographies, self-help books, pamphlets. If the word cancer was anywhere on the cover or jacket wording, I read it. My brother David and sister Ali acted as ferrets for me, buzzing around libraries and resource centres digging out material. I'm sure this search for information is familiar to many people who have to face a future with the disease. It's not only about being in a position to ask the right questions. It's a matter of knowing what you're dealing with, understanding the enemy.

As well as the information I was able to pick up from reading and talking to people, there were the letters I received from people who claimed to have cures and reliefs. Some were a bit wacky, but they provided leads to be explored. When there's the slightest chance that something might help save your life, there's no limit to your curiosity.

Initially my ignorance about cancer was almost boundless.

Above: Aged one and a bit, 1957.

Right: Does this count as my first car? Summer of 1957 with David.

Yes I know the grip is unconventional, but I'm expecting an awkward bounce. On holiday, aged four.

Not three wise monkeys – just David, Ali and me on the day the new telly arrived.

With David, Ali and assorted chickens in the garden at Batheaston, 1963.

A familiar holiday experience – drying out after a flood at Dockens Water in the New Forest. I'm in the woolly hat (*centre front*) flanked by David and my dad.

Drama was my third great love, after sport and art – joint production with the local boys school, circa 1973.

My classmates on the day we finished our O levels. I'm the grinning blackleg in the front row. Deb is next to me on the left stretching her legs.

With Tiger, our long-suffering cat, circa 1973.

My very first recorded interview – in Eastbourne town centre as part of a student project.

With my three college flatmates, 1977. (*Left to right*) me, Helen (Robs), Mandy and Nutch.

And the same four, twenty-one years later, Christmas 1998. (*Left to right*) Robs, Nutch, me and Mandy

Top of the Pops it isn't. Miming with Mandy in the Eastbourne flat.

With Nikki aged nine months, spring 1984.

Above: With John and Nikki, 1984.
Right: With Nikki and snow, Les Trois Vallées.
Below: My mum, Nikki, me and Ali, 1993.

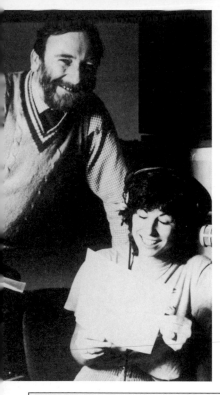

Above: In the *Newsround* studio, 1989.

Left: In the studio at Essex Radio with my boss Roger Buxton.

Below: My publicity shot for the 1990 Commonwealth Games.

Helen's Sporting
Chance

I didn't even know what an oncologist was until the day one came to see me. If the question had been thrown at me in a quiz, I would probably have guessed at something to do with pigs. So the diagnosis opened up a whole new world for me, like one of those secret doors in children's stories that fly open to reveal a hidden passageway when you press the right stone in the wall. When you're fit and healthy there is no particular reason to seek out the door. Looking back, I find it amazing that things which are now part of my daily routine were so strange to me.

Knowing what is happening is part of an ongoing campaign. Whatever treatment I'm having – blood test, chemo, whatever – I have to know exactly what it is all about, what it's aiming to achieve, what the risks and side effects are likely to be. I insist on it. From time to time a nurse may be a bit casual in setting up the chemo, and that irritates me beyond measure. I know what the stuff is doing to the tumours and what it's doing to me. If it's not absolutely right, then all the hassle, pain and fatigue is for nothing.

I am wary of offering advice to other cancer sufferers on the basis of my own experience. All our bodies and experiences are unique, and what works for me may not for somebody else. But I think its vital for anybody faced with a cancer diagnosis to find out all they can about their illness, and make sure they get the doctors to explain what they are proposing to do and what other options there are. It astonishes me when I come across people who act as if what is being done to their bodies is none of their business. 'I'm sure the doctor knows what he's doing,' they say.

This professional-knows-best attitude might be acceptable when the car or central heating goes on the blink, but where our own workings are concerned, we owe it to ourselves to get more involved. Doctors are not infallible and as patients we have one distinct edge over them. We're actually living in the malfunctioning bodies.

The doctors treating me have been great – always ready to take time with me, to listen, to explain, to consider alternatives. I've been incredibly lucky to meet such exceptional people. Most amazing is how personally committed they have been to my recovery. Their warmth and humanity has touched me greatly. None of the cool professional distance. When things have looked particularly black, we have even cried together. I have wondered at times how, with involvement like that, they manage to do the job.

I was surprised to discover how many approaches – orthodox and alternative – there are to alleviating and fighting cancer. Very confusing for the newcomer. The skirmishing which occurs across the orthodox/alternative border doesn't help much either. Faced with conflicting claims that standard treatments are of dubious value and that alternative therapies are worthless, the unfortunate patient can be left wondering what to do. Happily, my doctors were encouraging in respect of alternative treatments, and I found myself adopting a pick-and-mix approach among those that made the greatest sense to me. I am convinced that, whatever the treatment, the patient's attitude towards it is an important factor in its success. But you're unlikely to have a positive attitude towards your treatment unless you are working in partnership with your doctor or therapist, understanding and approving of what he or she is trying to do.

My first meeting with the oncologist Dr Neville Davidson was an auspicious start for a partnership. He pulled no punches. 'You could be in big trouble.' But he was not about to give up on me. With help from my two friends, we spent some time thrashing out what he could do for me, and at the end of it I asked him if he was an optimist. He said he was. Important to ask that question. I figured that in my condition a pessimistic doctor would be as much use as a steeplejack with vertigo. He was telling the truth. Time and again when we have hit difficulties, he has been ready to take a different tack, try a new approach. Deceptively laid back, unswervingly positive; as long as I'm prepared to carry on the struggle, he is right there with me.

Dr Davidson wasn't prepared to start my chemo right away. I needed a few more days to recover from my operations. By the time my first chemo session loomed on 22nd September I felt relaxed and prepared. Better than at any time since I went into hospital. In my diary I wrote, 'I'm up for the fight – ready to kill the little bastards that are invading my precious body.' Once again my good friend Hazel was there to help me through it. Dr Davidson whistled as he put the lethal bag up, as casual as if he was hanging out washing.

Reaction to the poison entering my veins was violent and immediate – sickness, diarrhoea, sweating, eye disturbance, salivating. Pretty horrible for about two and a half hours, but even at its worst I remember thinking to myself that it wasn't as bad as I had felt the previous week in the aftermath of the operation. Once the storm had passed I felt peaceful and triumphant. It was as if sunshine had entered my body. Very strange.

Where a tumour is located in a specific site, it is possible to use surgery or radiotherapy to eradicate it, but the problem with cancer is that it spreads through the lymph nodes to surrounding areas and then via the bloodstream to other parts of the body. This is what had happened in my case. A cancerous tumour in the colon had spread to the liver, and my initial scans showed twenty-two secondary tumours, with very little of the organ unaffected. So while the surgeons could remove the original colon tumour, they couldn't start hacking away at my liver in that condition. This is where chemotherapy comes in.

Chemotherapy is the use of drugs which circulate in the body and attack cancer cells wherever they occur. Most of the drugs work by inhibiting the normal division of cells, particularly those which are reproducing rapidly – a feature of cancer cells. Almost a million possible cancer-inhibiting substances have been tested over the years but only about fifty drugs are commonly in use. They act on different stages in the cell cycle, so oncologists will often use a combination of two or more drugs to maximise their effect. Using more than one drug may also allow them to be prescribed at a lesser strength, thus reducing side effects, and may also delay the onset of resistance. Over time, cancer cells, just like all the others in our bodies, build up a tolerance to toxic substances intended to zap them.

Initially I was treated with a combination of two drugs – campto and 5FU (I wonder who chose the names for them.) They were administered in a dilute form via a bag which fed them directly into a vein. This is the most common way of getting cancer drugs into the body, although it is possible to take some orally or have them injected. Ironically, the people handling the drugs have to be very careful not to come into contact with them, because they can actually cause cancer.

Freedom came quickly in the days that followed that first chemotherapy session. First the feedbag was removed. It was decided that I could manage to keep body and soul together in the normal way without being shackled to a bag of chow constantly drip-feeding through my neck. Yippee! I could move about, get the circulation going and hopefully avoid the horrid double bee sting of the nightly anti-clotting heparin jab.

Next day, I took my first trip outside. A walk, well more a drunken disoriented shuffle, in nearby Thornden Park – a friend on either arm to prevent me from pitching head first into the nearest flower bed. Could it really be just five weeks since I walked into the hospital? That life seemed like a distant dream. Going to the park was a part of re-entering the real world, but it was changed and so was I. I couldn't get over the smell of damp leaves, kept turning my head to sniff.

That night, Nikki was allowed to stay with me in hospital for the first time. Just wonderful to have her there. We talked, said a little prayer together and watched *An Audience with Elton John* on TV, raucously singing along to 'I'm Still Standing'. What we lacked in musical pitch, we more than made up in volume. Shame about the other patients, but I needed to bellow my good fortune. No song was ever more appropriate. I felt that I'd started to turn the corner – I was on the way back.

My second bout of chemo, a week after the first, was

less fearsome than I had expected and added to the sense of progress. No repeat of the previous week's nausea. I was even able to read the newspapers while it was being administered. Another positive sign was the return of my appetite for sport. My own plight began to take second place to excitement about Europe's narrow victory in the Ryder Cup. The commentary team rang me from Valderama. Almost as good as being there.

'You can go home on Friday.'

Scary! Suddenly I was worried. After just six weeks the hospital felt like home. The nurses did everything for me. Leaving meant managing for myself and I wasn't sure I could do it. What's more, I wasn't going home because I was better, fixed up and recovering from a broken leg or a car accident. The thing that had put me into hospital was still there – just under control for the moment. And the future? Uncertain to say the least. I cried when I left.

'Can't walk properly- I'm basically an invalid. Ten minutes standing up is all I can do. Will I cope? I must realise I have all the time in the world.'

What a strange thing for somebody who patently doesn't have all the time in the world to write in their diary. Was I in denial or just trying to be positive? I can't remember to be honest. Most probably the comment was simply a warning to myself not to be impatient for quick results. I was certainly aware of the seriousness of my condition. What I didn't find out until later was that at the end of August the doctors had given me just three months to live.

When you have just staggered out of hospital, some errands

take priority. Nikki, on her way from Brentwood Station to meet me, was horrified to spot me across the road buying wine in an off licence.

'What the hell are you doing?'

'Oh, it's not for me. Just a thank you for the nurses.'

Pity. Wouldn't mind a glass of wine.

The house was like a building site from the work that had started the day I left. Dust everywhere and work still unfinished. I guess I should have been grateful to have escaped six weeks of bum cleavage and fag ends outside the back door, but why is it that ever since Stonehenge, builders have always felt this need to leave jobs incomplete? Thank God for friends, yet again, who blitzed the place to make it liveable before I got back.

I was hardly through the door before the hassles of my new life hit me. They came in the shape of an officious district nurse (male) who seemed more concerned with getting his paperwork in order than with the state of my health. Unmoved by reminders that I had only just arrived home, and oblivious to some pretty strong body language, he trudged through an information-gathering routine until, all civility exhausted, we told him to sling his hook.

The overwhelming sensation was of life happening around me. Somehow I didn't seem to be a part of it all.

I'm disabled. Something which had never occurred to me. Sue, the lovely Macmillan nurse, suggested that I apply for disability parking stickers. What a surprise! Even at my lowest ebb I had thought of my illness as a temporary state. I would either recover or die. Orange stickers signified something else

41

– a permanent condition of disability that I had yet to take on board. My feeble protests were gently extinguished.

'How far can you walk?'

I got the stickers.

Cancer cells reproduce themselves at a very fast rate. Chemotherapy acts upon all fast-growing cells, so while it hits the cancer cells it also takes its toll on the élite sprinters among the other cells of the body. These include the skin, hair, lining of the mouth and intestine. Hair loss is the most visible and best-known result of this, but there are many others – sore mouth, sensitive skin, chronic diarrhoea. I had the lot, but none had quite the impact of the hair.

In preparation for the inevitable I had my hair cut to an inch and a half all over. Lawrence from the BBC came to do it specially. I told myself that I wasn't worried about my hair dropping out – painless, the only thing to be hurt will be my vanity. My self-reassurance didn't work. Nikki asked me if I was afraid of it, and I was about to say no when I just burst into tears.

It didn't happen until after the second chemo session – a very strong dose of campto. What a shock! Hair was all over the pillow, all over the bathroom. Despite my preparatory shearing it was everywhere, and you just couldn't get rid of it. There are around 150,000 individual hairs on the average human head, and I reckon that every one of mine tried to compensate for its treacherous willingness to leave my head by stubborn refusal to surrender to the Hoover.

Baldness seemed to accentuate the other effects of my illness and the weeks in hospital. The mirror presented me with the image of a scrawny little bird – tiny head with oversized features, bulging abdomen and weak stalky little legs – for all the world like one of those featherless specimens that make a habit of falling from nests in the early spring. It was utterly devastating. Without Nikki's help I would have had great difficulty coping with it. She boosted my confidence by showing me that my baldness was no problem for her – a very mature thing for a fourteen-year-old to do. She had no worries about being seen with her little bald mother, never once asked me to put on my wig when we went out together. I quickly learned to answer to my new name, 'Slaphead', and to respond to her good-natured banter. Others helped to bolster me, too. Andrew Thompson, the Breakfast News Editor at the BBC, encouraged me to come and present the Sports News without my wig. A lovely thought, but one which might have left the viewers choking on their cornflakes.

I became less self-conscious as the weeks went by, but it was a relief to find my hair growing back again. Losing it again in May was, if anything, harder than the first time. My tumour levels had reached crisis point and we had to go for the strong doses of campto again. It was horribly depressing to find myself back to square one, and just two days before I was due to go back on air after quite a long lay off.

I had read about ways of preventing hair loss during chemo-therapy. They sound rather bizarre – artificially cooling the head during the treatment or restricting the blood flow to the scalp with tight rubber bands. I talked them over with the doctor who advised me that such methods were pretty painful and expensive, not necessarily effective and potentially dangerous.

It seems that restricting the blood flow in this way could result in some cancer cells escaping, and you could be giving yourself real problems sending them all over your body. Ah well! Back to the wig and the head polish.

I decided to go for a pukka made-to-measure wig; important if I was going to get back to work. Anyway, my head's so small I would never have got an off-the-peg one to fit. The wig-maker was a dapper little man, Richard Mawby, who had resurfaced half the bonces in showbiz. That was comforting, but I was totally freaked when he brought the finished article.

'My God! I look like the Wild Woman of Borneo.'

'Don't worry, Helen, I've still to cut it to shape.'

Two and a half hours of fascinating gossip later, I had a smart new expensive hairstyle, and not a join to be seen.

I hated wearing it. It's good. It looks real, but it's someone else's hair, not mine. The first time I wore it on a trip into town, I was seized by an almost irresistible urge to tear it off and shout, 'Hey, look, this is me. This is where I'm at!'

In the weeks that followed my departure from hospital a familiar pattern established itself. Back in for chemo every week, a day or so to recover and pick myself up in time for the next bout. Each day brought a new round of visitors and the telephone rang constantly. People were so kind and concerned, but as time went on I began to crave a bit of peace. I needed their support, I appreciated their concern, but wouldn't it have been wonderful to have an on/off switch, or at least some way of storing up the love and kindness for when I particularly needed it? Some nights at 3 a.m. when cold fear swept through me, a friendly voice and hug, so plentiful during the day, would have made a world of difference. Of course, there were some people who wouldn't have minded me phoning them at three in the morning, but I couldn't have done it. They had jobs, families, lives of their own.

There were a few other people whose involvement with my plight seemed to have more to do with boosting their own egos than with helping me, but they were such a tiny minority. Most people took incredible time and trouble over me without wanting anything in return. I felt so lucky and guilty for being lucky. I had received so much but wasn't doing anything for others, hadn't even responded yet to hundreds of letters and good wishes sent to me when I was in hospital. The BBC came to my rescue with the offer of secretarial help to clear the backlog.

My life was entirely dominated by the illness. Clear in my mind was the objective of getting tumour levels down to a point where I could undergo a liver operation, and I put all my energies into achieving it. In addition to the conventional treatment I was receiving I followed up a variety of alternative therapies – Chinese medicine, acupuncture, the strictest of food regimes courtesy of Terry Moule, a naturopath recommended to me by one of the hundreds of people who wrote in the early days. By the end of October my tumour levels were down by half and the doctors were describing my progress as nothing short of miraculous. When you are adopting a variety of treatments it's impossible to say which is doing the most good, but with progress like this I was not about to give up on anything. Appointments, treatments, pills, recipes, I approached them all with the discipline of a zealot.

The petty crises of normal life don't go away when you're ill. You can be shielded from them in hospital, but back home they shout for attention on top of everything else. And strangely, it is often the trivial things that keep you awake at night. Like bathrooms – yeah, that's right. How can I be facing extinction and yet lying awake worrying about the sodding bathroom? Remember the unfinished building work? Anybody who has ever embarked on a property conversion or extension will know what a potent source of stress building work can be. But worrying about this stuff in my situation seemed ridiculous. It's two in the morning and I'm stirring away at a pot of resentment about a malfunctioning shower. Perhaps I need worry in small easily digested portions if I'm going to handle it. Just as my liver would give up the ghost if faced with a banquet, my brain wants simple everyday things to latch onto, because the uncertainty of my future is too much to contemplate. Or maybe it's just that I'm lacking other practical distractions – work for example. Yes perhaps that's it – must get back to work soon.

People at the BBC were keen to talk about my return. No shortage of possibilities in the New Year. Saturday evening sports roundup, some work for Breakfast, a possible trip to the winter Paralympics in March. Provided I was up to it, they were prepared to take a risk with me.

I was ambivalent. Recovery was occupying so much of my time and energy and was such a roller coaster. Just when I seemed to be making brilliant progress, I would be plunged into bitter awareness of my frailty. Self-confidence followed the same pattern – one day determined, the next weepy. In mid-November my first trip back into the broadcasting world

– as one of the judges for *The Sunday Times* Sportswoman of the Year – had been nerve-racking and exhausting. On the other hand, a return to work felt like the right thing to be doing. Cancer hadn't knocked the workaholic out of me. I was addicted to lists, plans and schedules. Sitting in the garden reading a book wouldn't be enough to keep me going. I had to get back to work.

In early December I went to town Christmas shopping and came back to find the house ransacked. Jewellery, Christmas presents, video, CDs, the satellite dish (odd thing to steal) all gone. Nothing irreplaceable, nothing of enormous value, but a huge sense of having been violated. 'What's going on? I can do without this. Bastards!'

As if to add to the shitty deal, the *News of the World* turned up on the doorstep – there had been an anonymous call to their office to say that I'd been burgled. 'God! surely this can't be news.' Police trundled in and out taking statements and checking for fingerprints. For days I felt vulnerable and afraid. Nikki and I slept in the same bed too frightened to be alone in a bedroom. Only after spending a small fortune on a new alarm and security locks did we start to relax. It's a common response after a burglary, I know. But it felt like the final straw. 'What next for God's sake?'

I wanted to get away for Christmas, to be pampered and to spend what might well be my final festive season with members of my family. We agreed upon a hotel at Saunton Sands in North Devon that could meet my dietary requirements. I wanted it to be a very special time. The hotel was lovely, perched on the cliffs overlooking the bay. Nice to be looked after, and great to have my family around me, but a disappointment in other ways. Christmas is so much about eating and drinking. I felt resentful that I couldn't tuck into the available scoff. The few titbits I allowed myself made me feel unwell and incredibly guilty. And although we never said so, I think the knowledge that this might be my last Christmas put a dampener on the occasion.

New Year was worse. Two of my best friends spent New Year's Eve with me and we all made resolutions about remaining positive, but 1998 scared me. It was going to be a make or break year. Despite all the love and support I had received, I felt lonely and depressed. In my diary I wrote, 'If it wasn't for Nikki, frankly I wouldn't care if I lived or died.' I cheered myself up by pulling out the last remaining stitches from my operation. What a relief! The spiky end sticking out of my abdomen had been causing me grief for weeks. I taped the six-inch length of blue nylon into my diary as a reminder.

They say that the Samaritans have to lay on special troops for New Year. I can understand it. It brings you starkly up against past failings and future fears.

'Come on, H. Pull yourself together. Beating this thing is all about attitude.'

I did it by plunging myself back into work. I sorely missed the discipline, the buzz and the structure it gave my life. Was I ready? Well, they were prepared to sling me in front of the cameras again – so let's give it a go. I phoned them to say that I was ready to go back on 10th January.

All hell broke loose. The *Sun*, which had been badgering for a story for some time, ran a front-page piece, 'Brave Helen

Back To Work'. Other reporters beat a path to my door and Breakfast TV turned up outside my house with their satellite van to beam me live into the programme. The phone became as insistent as a hungry infant. It was all rather startling and out of control. I didn't feel particularly brave, and I wasn't trying to prove anything by going back to work. It was just something I needed to do. After all the years I still get a tremendous buzz of excitement every time I go into a TV studio or an outside broadcast van.

On 10th January I gave myself plenty of time to get ready, but ended up rushing around the house. That's normal, but the nerves weren't. I fumbled and fussed over my preparation, gobbled my lunch.

'Hey you're just going back to work. After what you've been through, this is nothing.'

It was great to see everybody *Grandstand, Match of the Day* and News teams. Lots of people phoned to wish me luck, there were heaps of cards and messages on the computer. I began to get anxious. Out of practice as I was, and with all the interruptions, would I be able to write my material in time? We had a run through at 6.15 – something we had never done before. I was relieved to discover that I could still read the autocue. I guess that everyone else was, too. Jenny the make-up artist gave me a plant and checked my make-up. On air at last, Chris Lowe, the newsreader, introduced me with the words, 'And now for a full roundup of today's sport, we are delighted to welcome back Helen Rollason.'

I presented my piece – no stumbles. It felt as if I had just woken up from a bad dream. So strange and almost surreal to be there after so long. And yet it also felt as if I had never been away.

4

Getting on to the Box

'All you need in life is ignorance and confidence, then success is sure.'

MARK TWAIN

I DECIDED that I wanted to work in television at the age of eight and never really deviated from that ambition. But I can't say that I ever got much encouragement. Careers teachers in those days were positively scornful of aspirations they viewed as unrealistic, probably still are for all I know, and my family had no media background or connections. I was a personable teenager, mad about sport, good at drama and art, but not particularly academic. Careers advice? Teaching, of course.

So that's what I did. It was a perfectly reasonable choice. My television ideas were a bit pie in the sky, and at that time there wasn't the range of sport-related opportunities there are now. I specialised in PE and had a brilliant time training at Chelsea College in Eastbourne. But the TV thing didn't go away. While still at college I wrote to the BBC, said I wanted to present *Blue Peter*. My big idea was that sport could feature more prominently in the programme and that, realising this, the Beeb would decide that I was just the person they needed to deliver it.

They didn't. I received a standard polite photocopied response. One young hopeful among hundreds. I gave TV ambitions a couple of years rest, finished at college and took a job in a Winchester comprehensive. But before long there it was again.

Can't imagine doing this for the rest of my life.

I started looking at the BBC job advertisements.

When I look back, I cringe at my naivety. I had no idea what was involved in TV presentation. I thought it was just a matter of looking at the camera and saying some vaguely relevant things. But my ignorance didn't stop me from applying. Perhaps it helped. If I'd appreciated what talented people I was up against, I might have been too daunted to try. I applied for a sports presentation job with BBC Wales. Got an audition. Wow! Here we go.

As part of the process candidates were asked to interview a sports person. They stuck this guy in front of me and told me to get on with it. The face looks familiar, but who the hell is he? I spent most of the interview trying to uncover his identity. It was more like a game of *What's My Line?* than a sports interview. I ascertained he was something to do with rugby union, and went in with my killer question.

'So what is your contribution to rugby?'

Out of the corner of my eye I could see that the cameramen were finding something amusing – well, almost crying with laughter to be honest – but it didn't put me off. I thought that if they were so appreciative it must be going really well. I found out afterwards that I had been interviewing Carwyn James, the renowned British Lions coach, credited with masterminding the most successful Lions tour ever, and arguably the biggest contributor to British rugby at the time.

I'm not sure whether it was humane or cruel of them not to kick me out there and then. They let me go on to the next test, a piece of video footage to which candidates were required to provide a commentary. Routine, bread and butter stuff which nowadays I could do standing on my head. That's if I could stand on my head, which at the moment I can't. I hadn't the foggiest idea how to set about it. I thought you just said anything that came into your head. I burbled a string of unconnected thoughts and came away quite pleased with myself. That must have given them quite a laugh, too.

So I didn't get that job, and nor was I any more successful in another try out I had at BBC South.

On this occasion I had a nasty attack of foot and mouth. I was asked to write a script and deliver it to camera. The script wasn't too bad as I recall, but I wasn't ready for the mechanics of delivering it. The autoscript relied on a foot pedal which you operated to move the script along at the right speed for your delivery. Any learner driver or novice sewing machine operator will know the problem. Either it wouldn't move at all or it went like the clappers. I just couldn't get the speed right and most of the time was gabbling like a racing commentator in the final furlong just to keep up.

Never mind. Perhaps teaching isn't that bad after all.

My future husband lived in Essex, and I gave up my teaching job in Winchester to move there, got hold of some supply teaching, but knew I didn't want to teach for much longer. My broadcasting failures hadn't discouraged me, I was still up for any opportunity. One day in Basildon town centre I saw a notice saying 'Basildon Community Radio'. I just walked in and asked if I could help.

'Can you write?'

'Umm, I think so. I want to do some sport.'

'Well you can't just do sport. You'll have to be prepared to do some ads as well and a bit of news.'

'OK.'

'And it's all voluntary, by the way.'

Basildon Community Radio went out through cable to thousands of houses in the town as part of an early cable television package. Whether anybody listened to it, I never quite discovered. But, boy did I get the chance to do some different things! I found myself writing adverts – 'If your tyres let you down, try Autotread, the best in town'– and voicing them as well. I wrote and presented news, and had a field day with sport. I listened to my voice coming from the television set and thought, 'God, I've made it!' Essex was absolutely buzzing with sports stars at that time and I went off to interview scores of them just by saying that I was from Basildon Community Radio. If you abbreviated the station's name to BC Radio and stammered over the first initial, you could make yourself sound really important, but I never needed to. Stars who these days can only be approached through an agent with a £1000 price tag would quite happily let themselves be quizzed for free by a twenty-four-year-old amateur hack with no experience whatsoever. How times have changed.

After a few months of voluntary broadcasting, combined with enough teaching to keep the wolf from the door, I decided a bit of career development was in order. I took shorthand and typing qualifications and looked around for the next step. If I was really lucky, somebody might actually be prepared to pay me for doing this kind of thing.

It was the time when the local commercial radio stations were starting to be set up. Essex Radio advertised that they were coming on the air. So I went grovelling to them offering to do anything – clean the floors, anything.

'Sorry, love. We've already appointed everybody.'

I must have made quite a nuisance of myself because eventually they let me in and paid me about £50 a week as a dogsbody's assistant. It wasn't quite cleaning the floors but I had to do a bit of everything – secretarial work and general admin. But I did get some of what I really wanted, helping out on Saturday afternoons with the sport.

Within a few months they gave me the job of Deputy Sports Editor. Impressive title, but no inflated salary to match. I was still on £50 a week and working incredible hours. Pretty soon I was presenting a Saturday afternoon sports show. The format was a sport and music sandwich – record, bit of sport, record – and the presenter had to operate the equipment as well as handling the sports news, features and interviews. Brilliant training for coping with a live broadcast while simultaneously thinking about six other things. With so many things to juggle there were inevitable errors.

On one occasion I introduced a record by Buck's Fizz, an error in itself you might say, but worse was to come. I intended to say Buck's Fizz, but somehow, like one of those tongue-twisters used in drinking games, I managed to swap the initial letters of the group's name. Whoops! It sounds pretty tame by today's standards, but in 1981 definitely taboo, especially on a Saturday afternoon. I recoiled from the microphone in horror as if Mary Whitehouse was about to leap out of it to give me a good thrashing. I imagined that the whole of Essex had heard it and waited in trepidation for a flood of complaints. Nothing happened. Either nobody noticed, or nobody was listening, or nobody cared.

In 1981 there were no women doing sports presentation, so I felt as if I was breaking new ground. My editor, Roger Buxton, liked to hang on to the cricket and football, but he was happy to give me a free hand with most other things, so I had a wonderful time being really creative and pushing quite a lot of sports in the county. I could do more or less everything I wanted and Essex had world champions in God knows how many sports. There are people now almost retiring from their sports whom I have interviewed right through their careers.

Essex Radio gave me a great kick start. I had taken a major drop in salary to move from teaching into this new precarious world, but looking back on it I think I knew what I was doing. It felt like a risk at the time, but if it had all gone pear-shaped, I guess I could have got back into teaching easily enough. The job was what I wanted to be doing, and in those circumstances, as long as you can eat, salary is not too important.

In the summer of 1983 I had to take a break. Motherhood

beckoned. In any event it felt like the right time to be leaving. I had learned a great deal in a short time at Essex, but I decided that when I was ready to go back to work, it would be to another station, possibly IRN or one of the other independent stations in London.

The following spring, with Nikki nine months old, I felt ready to pick up the threads. I looked around and saw an assistant producer's job with a small television company called Cheerleader, which produced mainly American sport for Channel 4. New experience, could be interesting. I applied.

There was a lot of male chauvinism in the sports media world at the time. I suspect that the Managing Director regarded an application from a young married woman as something of an amusing novelty. He asked me if my ambition was to be the Anna Ford of sport.

'Oh, no,' I lied. 'I just want to work behind the scenes.'

Either he believed me or he knew a good line when he heard one. I got the job and learned some very quick lessons about television production and direction. The first lesson – not everything about television is glamorous – came on day one. One of my first tasks was to log some recorded American Football – every shot.

'Hey, there are several shots a minute here, and I've got hours of the stuff to do.'

'Welcome to television.'

I had never worked so hard in my life. Anybody coming into a small production company like that would have been under pressure. There were so few of us and we produced so much television. Schedules were much tighter than in larger outfits, which meant that you were constantly up against it. For somebody who was trying to learn the business, prove that they could hack it and manage life with a young child, it was almost too much. Assignments would fall on your desk at the shortest of notice. 'You're going to New York tomorrow to do the US Open.' Or 'You're on the Davis Cup for the next couple of weeks.' You would be expected to drop everything and just go.

I did it. Proving to myself and others that I could was important. I can't quit. It's a bad thing, and I suspect that the stress of trying to do too much over a number of years may have contributed to my health problems. Ironically though, the same stubborn tendency that helped land me in my present situation, has assisted me in managing it. There have been many times in the last two years when I've felt like giving up. Times when I've felt so weary of trying, and I've thought, 'Why can't I just go to sleep and that will be it?' But within seconds I'm saying to myself, 'Don't you dare to be so selfish.' Quitting feels like letting myself and others down.

I was only with Cheerleader for a little over a year, but it gave me a grounding in production and direction which would have taken much longer in a larger organisation. For all my assurances about wanting to work behind the scenes, I was hungry to get out in front of the camera. I felt confident I could handle TV sports presentation, but it meant taking a bit of a risk again and becoming a freelancer.

In summer 1985 I gave up the role of employee and turned freelance. Those outside the television business are sometimes surprised to learn that the vast majority of presenters – all the big names – are freelancers rather than employees of the television companies. I approached Thames Sport and Channel 4 and got myself some work. I remember the first assignment I had in front of the camera was a piece on judo. It involved an enormous team of more than a dozen because of all the snipping and cutting required to assemble it.

I guess that first job was a milestone in my career. At last I was doing what I had always wanted to do. But it didn't feel particularly important at the time – more of a transition from radio presentation and TV production than a bold leap in the dark.

The amount of sports presentation I could get my hands on was initially quite limited, so I needed other things to supplement it. I saw a BBC advert for a reporter with John Craven's *Newsround*. It looked like something which I could do at the same time as developing my sport, and might provide some useful experience in a new area. I knew the programme well and decided that with my sports experience I would be able to bring a new dimension to the programme, there was really no coverage of young people's sport at the time. As the marketing people would say, I made sport my Unique Selling Proposition, and got the job.

Newsround had been a feature of BBC Children's television since the early seventies. It was, incidentally, the world's first children's television news programme. Aiming at a target audience of eight- to twelve-year-olds, it sought, and still seeks, to cover news stories of particular interest to children, and to present the main news of the day in a way that children will find intelligible. Background knowledge cannot be assumed, as it can in adult news broadcasts, and this educational element appealed .

to the not quite forgotten teacher in me. Presenting some of the historic stories of the 1980s in a way that was informative and intelligible was not without challenge. I remember at the time the Berlin Wall came down, writing a piece which attempted to summarise the whole of Eastern European history since the Russian Revolution in one and half minutes.

John Craven had fronted the programme since 1972, and when I joined was still the main presenter. Gradually over the late eighties the balance changed. Roger Finn, who joined around the same time as me, and I took an increasing share and, when John left in 1989, we became the two main presenters. As on every news programme there were occasional disagreements about approach, but on the whole there was a genial and co-operative atmosphere among the team.

Although *Newsround* was produced by the Children's Department, it worked closely with BBC News which provided the programme with access to its reporters, correspondents and facilities. In fact, because of the timing of the programme, it was sometimes the first bulletin to break big stories. The Challenger shuttle disaster in 1986 was an occasion in point.

My four and a half years with the programme provided me with a really broad journalistic experience that would have been difficult to obtain elsewhere. But the thing that most interested me about the *Newsround* job was the opportunity to introduce young people's sport to TV. By the time I left all the contacts were in place to provide full coverage of a whole range of sports. It helped that during the latter part of my time on *Newsround* I was simultaneously presenting for BBC and ITV Sport. It meant that I was able to keep my finger on the pulse, and knew who were the youngsters we needed to keep our eyes on. I can remember interviewing the sprinter Katherine Merry when she was an eleven-year-old, and wondering whether she would make the transition to senior level. She did, and recently set a British indoor record for the 200 metres in Birmingham.

Newsround Extra has been one of the abiding features of the programme – fifteen-minute documentaries looking at issues in greater depth than was possible in the five-minute bulletin. One of these, a programme I directed on the plight of the street children of Bogota, provided the starkest imprint on my memory of those years. We went to Colombia, taking an eleven-year-old British girl who had won a competition to make the film. We all knew that we were going to see some tragic sights, but the experience was ten times more heartbreaking than we could have imagined It was particularly traumatic for the girl through whose eyes we were making the film.

Even as we drove into the city from the airport, we were shocked to see small humps of tattered rags curled in doorways and gutters, and slightly more animate little figures picking over huge piles of festering rubbish, children as young as five living and dying on the streets. It is reckoned that, in Latin America, there are some 10 million children who live their lives exclusively on the streets. They are known as 'the disposable ones'.

The problem has its origins in the burgeoning urban popula-tions throughout South America. In an effort to escape grinding rural poverty, exploitation or political violence, ever increasing numbers migrate to the cities in the hope of employment and a better life. The prospect turns out to be an illusion. There may be wealth in the cities but it doesn't come in the direction of the illiterate and unskilled. They make their homes in the sprawling shanties and set about surviving as best they can; thousands upon thousands of families, each crammed into a one-roomed shack surrounded by muddy squalor. In this environment, family structures and social networks break down. Violence and abuse are endemic.

Children end up on the street after being abandoned by their parents or escaping from domestic violence. They live under the streets as well as in them, sheltering in the sewers at night, and are particularly vulnerable to abuse. Many are sexually exploited or are drawn into criminal gangs, and there is a worrying tendency in a number of South American cities towards large-scale child killings by vigilante groups and members of the police forces in the name of urban cleansing. An estimated 95 per cent of Bogota's street children use drugs to escape the pain and hunger of their existence. Usually this means glue- or petrol-sniffing with its potential for long-term brain, lung and kidney damage. Add this to the malnutrition, chronic bronchitis, injury and disease which affects these kids, and you have a recipe for a short miserable life.

And yet for all this mean, de-humanising existence, they are still just children with the curiosity and affection of children everywhere. For part of the film I needed to do a piece to camera, which we shot on one of the enormous rubbish dumps. The children crowded round, trying to hold my hand, and for the only time in my professional career I just burst into tears.

Showing emotion on screen is something a news presenter doesn't do. When you are trying to get a message across which you hope will make a difference to viewers' knowledge and attitudes, the last thing they need is you blubbing. You need to be able to say to yourself, 'Hold on! If I can't do this professionally, people won't know what's happening here.' Normally, I have been able to do it, but I got caught out on that occasion. You might imagine that being able to turn off your emotions like this makes you into a colder, harder person, but observing some of the really great news presenters, as I have over the years, I don't think that's true. In BBC News I have met some of the most caring people anywhere, and they are deeply affected by the stories they have to cover.

Of course, I did get the piece to camera done, and I was very proud of the finished film which looked at the situation through the eyes of the youngster we had taken with us, and the actions of charities and individuals who were attempting to make a difference.

But the experience anaesthetised my emotions for a long time afterwards. I couldn't really grieve for anybody who had enjoyed a fulfilling life and a normal life span, because nothing was as bad as the life these children were having. I still measure my own situation against that experience and recognise that, even though I may be dying, I've had an absolutely brilliant life by comparison. It stops me feeling sorry for myself.

In the late eighties I had my feet in several camps. I had been able to move on from the production work with Cheerleader into freelance sports presentation for ITV and Channel 4, and was keeping this up at the same time as working for *Newsround*. The Head of BBC Sport spotted me beetling away for ITV at the Seoul Olympics and was apparently impressed by my work-rate. I found myself in the unprecedented position of presenting sport for both the BBC and the independent channels.

At this and other stages in my career there were alternative routes that I might have taken, but there was no doubt in my mind that presenting sport for the BBC was the one I wanted. I had enjoyed my time at *Newsround* very much, but it was clear that I couldn't remain there much longer. In my mid-thirties I was getting a bit too long in the tooth. At the time the fashion was for children's presenters who came over as trendy young parents. Much over thirty-five and you no longer fitted the bill. It has all changed now. The fashion today is for children's presenters who have just lost their milk teeth.

As for news reporting, I did a little in my early period in radio, but it's really not my scene. So much of it is to do with human misery, intruding on people at times of distress. With sports presentation it's a different matter. You can revel in the excitement and joy of the event. I guess that the wish to transmit enthusiasm and make people happy is one of the main reasons why sports presentation has always been my first love.

So I left *Newsround* – signed off with a report about the Cup Final replay – and committed myself full time to sport. It wasn't difficult to do. I had just been offered the biggest opportunity of my career, the chance to present *Grandstand*, the first woman to do so.

I took it, of course, but there was no preparation for the job. I leapt from one-off freelance assignments to anchoring the flagship of BBC Sport. It was a very big weight to carry and I almost didn't appreciate how important it was in the history of broadcasting. I was completely in awe of the people I was going to be working with. Rather than taking it by the scruff of the neck and saying I can do this, I was terrified.

When I walked into Television Centre on that day of my first *Grandstand* and all the security guards saluted, it didn't add to my confidence, just frightened me more. There was an air of naivety about me. I didn't realise beforehand what it was going to be like. Anchoring a full afternoon was a very different matter from the short pieces I had been used to. But then if I had known what it was going to be like, I might have been too frightened to do it. This really was the grown-up world of broadcasting and I wasn't quite ready for it.

Some people weren't quite ready for me either. One day I was presenting *Newsround* and the very next day, *Grandstand*. There were those who wondered what on earth the BBC was doing putting a children's presenter into this plum role. Unfortunately, nobody explained to them that I had ten years experience in sports broadcasting. The misconception remained, and got me off to a bad start.

What should have been the pinnacle of my career turned into a tough old time. I felt as if I hardly had a friend in the place, and I was too proud, frightened or stupid to ask for help. I guess that to some I appeared to think I knew it all. The opposite was true, but life is all about appearances.

In truth the first two or three *Grandstands* I did went quite well, but then came Wimbledon and that was another matter. I was asked if I would cover the women's tournament at Eastbourne the week before, and agreed, not realising that I had any choice in the matter. Unfortunately, I was the victim of crossed wires within the department, because the Wimbledon production team expected me for rehearsals during that same week. By the time I arrived at Wimbledon, knackered after Eastbourne, I had unwittingly put some people's backs up and reinforced a perception that I considered rehearsal unnecessary. Nothing could have been further from the truth. I was desperate for an opportunity to get on top of this job. Tennis was not one of my main strengths, and I realised with a pang of horror that I was expected to anchor not just the highlights programme for each day, but the whole thing. Eight hours of live broadcasting every day for a fortnight!

The word 'nightmare' trips too easily off the pen. I need something stronger to describe the two weeks of sheer hell that was Wimbledon 1990. Even now the thought of it makes me want to weep. I was up till all hours researching and preparing material, frantically going over it in the car, and marooned in a wretched cabin throughout the period of play, hardly even able to go to the loo. And all the while I had the awareness that I was failing.

My personal life at the time didn't help. My health had been playing up and severe endometriosis had been diagnosed, my marriage was falling apart, and that same week my mother had gone into hospital for a serious operation. Add to that the daily juggling and struggling with arrangements for a young child, and you have a less than ideal situation in which to take on the biggest professional challenge of your life.

Wimbledon felt like the first serious failure in my career, and what made it especially hard was the belief that, given different circumstances, I could have made a much better fist of it. Being thrown in at the deep end is all very well, but until you get your confidence, a buoyancy aid does help. I'm pleased to see that more recent entrants to high-profile anchoring jobs have had much more in the way of preparation than I received.

There's no doubt that my career took a knock after the Wimbledon experience. For quite a while I had to be content with covering less popular events, and I never quite recaptured the high ground that seemed to be there for the taking in 1990. I'm not bitter about that. It's one of those things which happens in life. I'm pleased that there are now many more women in TV sports presentation and, without blowing my own trumpet too loudly, I am prepared to take some small credit for helping to blaze a trail.

Over the next couple of years I rebuilt my confidence, developed those areas that particularly interested me – athletics and disability sport remain my favourites – and started to present sport on News and Breakfast. BBC News and Sport came to feel like home to me, and people who seemed so awesome at the time I joined, I would now count among my dearest friends. There are one or two people I find it hard to feel charitable towards, but that's not for now.

In the spring of 1996 my boss on Breakfast, Duncan Jones, told me that our editor had taken a table at the Television and Radio Industries Awards and invited the two of us as a way of saying thank you for the general improvement in Breakfast Sports coverage since we had been involved with it. I was puzzled by the invitation. I could understand Duncan being there, but why me? It was only when we were at the event and I looked at the programme that I discovered my name was in the frame for Sports Presenter of the Year. I looked across at Duncan and he smirked like a small boy caught scrumping apples. The shock of nomination was followed pretty swiftly by the knowledge that I'd won, and any sense of having been duped disappeared under a great wave of affection.

I still love television. It's so exciting and I sometimes get cross with some of the younger lads and girls who are coming into it today and don't seem to feel that buzz. For me it brought together everything that was important – those things that enthused me even as a school kid. Art, drama and sport – it has aspects of all three, and I get the most enormous kick out of creating a piece of work, writing, editing and filming it. I'm given quite a lot of freedom to do that, perhaps because of my early experience in direction and production. It took a while to get to the point where I was happy and confident doing the things that I wanted to do, but it all came together beautifully at some stage and it has been the right profession for me.

5

January to April 1998

T HE phone is ringing in my dream. No it's ringing in the real world outside my dream and I'm struggling up through layers of sleep to answer it.

'Who? Oh, the *Daily Mail*.' (I resist the urge to swear at him.) 'No, I'm afraid it isn't convenient. It's Sunday morning; you've just woken me up; and I didn't get home from work until after midnight.'

I stand there like a bemused monk – dressing gown, minimal hair. Well, that was a good way to make sure I didn't bask for too long in the euphoria of my return to work. Fitting that the call should have come from my least favourite newspaper of the moment. I hadn't yet forgiven them for the errors in the story they ran when I was first ill.

The days that followed my reappearance on the box in January 1998 were marked by further phone calls and 'plucky Helen' stories that seemed to snowball through the tabloid week. But I felt even less plucky than I had the week before. The chemo that week made me very sick, turned my face bright red and left me feeling drunk and confused. More of my eyebrows and eyelashes were dropping out, but at least I had a smidgen of hair on my head, a quarter of an inch perhaps. How long would it take at this rate to grow a decent headful? In the bathroom I found some shampoo that promised added volume. Used it. No difference.

It appeared that BT had received a request for my phone to be disconnected. Bizarre! I had cursed the instrument a million times in recent weeks. Was this a telepathic break-through? Perhaps I needed to be more careful with my curses in future. Ought I to find out whether that *Daily Mail* reporter has gone down with a mystery illness?

The doctors were talking seriously about a liver operation in the next couple of months. It scared the hell out of me, but it was where my hopes of recovery lay. If they were confident, I must be. Scans and consultations with Mr Myrddin Rees, the specialist liver surgeon, were scheduled for the end of January and beginning of February.

Work was tough. I felt knackered from the chemo, anxious about the operation and depressed by my appearance. My contact lenses kept misting over on air. A bit disconcerting when you are struggling to read the autocue. My mother asked me whether something could be done about my frown. One day I nearly didn't go in, but I didn't want to let people down. A new pain patch, paracetamol and herbs saw me through. As I travelled in, a guy on the train said, 'Well done! We're so proud of you.' That probably did me as much good as the drugs.

My first meeting with Mr Rees brought me sharply up against the realities of my situation. I asked him whether I would die if I didn't have the operation, and he said I would.

For all the pain and drama, the ups and downs of the chemo, it could only offer me some extra time. Surgery was my only hope of major remission or recovery. The knowledge that my very life depended on this operation weighed heavily upon me.

At least I could be confident that I was going to the number one guy. Mr Rees had a national reputation. I heard he saved Willie Carson's life, among others. It was obvious that Mr R had quite an ego and it occurred to me that medical stars are not a lot different in that respect from those in media and showbiz. But what a gorgeous charming man. Are all surgeons like this or am I just exceptionally lucky?

Scans carried out at my local hospital showed continuing improvement, but the decision on whether an operation was possible would depend on detailed tests at Mr Rees's hospital in Basingstoke. My sister Ali drove there with me which was comforting, but I missed the friendly Hartswood Hospital and my familiar nurses. After fasting overnight I was plied with dubious substances from all angles. A litre of contrast to drink, painkillers in both ends, and fluid pumped into an artery in the groin. All designed to show in detail the scale of tumour activity in the liver. Various pictures were taken and I was required to lie flat for eight hours. Eventually at 4.30, I was wheeled to the loo, because I simply demanded it.

Waiting for the result was agonising. Mr Rees came into my room around 5 p.m. Two nurses were with him but I hardly noticed them. He sat on the bed near me and told me that nodules had been found in the clear patches of my liver. Surgery seemed out of the question. I could hear Ali crying.

Mr Rees said he wasn't going to throw in the towel, and

had arranged an MRI scan with a Harley Street specialist just in case his scans were not giving a true picture. But he also looked skywards and said, 'We need Him to give us a break.' It's pretty frightening when your doctor is seeking assistance from God.

I took the news calmly, flipped into professional mode once again. But as soon as he had left the room we sobbed, and later, after Ali went, I cried myself to sleep. This was desperate stuff. For months the possibility of an operation had hung before me, the gold medal in my personal Olympics. It gave me something to work towards, to believe in; a chance of liberation from this wretched disease. Now that had all been snatched away and the bleakness of my future was shockingly exposed. My life was really on the line now. Within the next few months I was probably going to die.

But what a difference a couple of days can make. A conversation with Mr Ribeiro, the surgeon who carried out my original colon operation, lifted my spirits. He explained there was a chance that fluid used in the scans might be pooling in holes in the liver left by tumours which chemotherapy had zapped. This could be giving a false indication of the extent to which tumours had spread. The MRI scan offered some hope after all, and I had something positive to get hold of once again. With this more hopeful explanation deposited in my survival account, I went off for a pleasant lunch with Des Lynam and, hey presto, I was almost back to my old self again.

The MRI scan was scheduled for Thursday 12th February. Well I'm glad they set the appointment for that day rather than the next. That really would be the final straw.

Magnetic Resonance Imaging, to use the full title, requires the victim to lie in a long tube surrounded by a strong magnetic field. Changes in the magnetic field are analysed to produce a picture of the internal structures of the body. The equipment for this type of scan is more complex and expensive than the more common CT scan, but can give a more accurate assessment of any abnormalities. I was expecting the experience to be uncomfortable. Claustrophobic is the description most people use. And yes, the fit was snug to say the least. 'Glad I'm not overweight.'

Most disturbing was the noise; as if half a dozen workmen with pneumatic drills were trying to break through the casing. The panic button mischievously challenged me to press it, but I forced myself to ignore it. After what seemed like an age, I was let out, only to find that the results were inconclusive, and that an injection of dye was needed to make my liver show up better on the screen. Back into the tube like a human torpedo for another round of ear-bashing.

Friday 13th was unbelievably warm for February – temperatures in the mid-sixties. I had expected to feel rough after the rigours of the previous day, but I felt marvellous. I prepared to hit my first serious golf ball in seven months. My partner was Tracy Harte another cancer patient who had bounced into my hospital room the previous autumn and lifted my spirits with her energy and enthusiasm for life. We set a new trend on the course with our smooth scalps. I couldn't match Tracy's power and accuracy, but I felt full of life, ready for anything. Over a cup of tea after the game, we were congratulating each other on how well we had coped with illness, when in ran a woman golfer, clearly distressed and on the edge of panic.

'Whatever is the matter?'

'I've just broken a nail.'

That evening Mr Rees phoned to tell me he was prepared to attempt surgery. It would be breaking new ground but he thought he could remove 95 per cent of the tumours. There would be three left in the good area of liver, and they would need to be tackled by cryosurgery, laser treatment or chemotherapy once the liver had been able to regenerate itself. Two-thirds of the liver would go in a three-stage surgical process, and along with it tumours in the right side which were the size of a grapefruit. As the liver that was left regenerated, growing back to its previous size, it would stretch the remaining tumours so that they could be dealt with more easily.

Mr Rees wasn't promising anything. Again when I went to see him the following day, he emphasised the ground-breaking nature of the operation. It was the only real option to prolong my life. His face was optimistic, what a contrast to the last time we had met a couple of weeks previously. I felt for the first time in seven months that we were going to crack it. I had prayed a lot that week and felt that my prayers had been answered. The number one liver specialist in the country was prepared to go ahead with an operation. Two weeks to eat well and get fit. I was up for it.

Easier said than done. I was slowly coming to the conclusion that my body wasn't what it used to be. I played a set of tennis with a friend and won 6–4, but I couldn't escape the sneaking feeling that she had let me win to boost my confidence. Would

I have done the same for her? Afterwards, my joints creaked like floorboards in a Hammer Horror film. Another day I went to the gym but the mere sight of the apparatus made me wilt. Nikki took a swim while I puffed and groaned my way around the chromium plated torture chamber.

'Well, perhaps that wasn't too bad after all.'

We moved on to the golf driving range, but my meagre supply of energy had dried up. After half a dozen balls I was done for.

Fitness and appearance have always been important to me. Maintaining tight muscles into my forties and never being more than a size 10 were matters of pride. It wasn't a great struggle; I loved my exercise. So the knowledge that I would never get my body back to what it was came hard. I'm still finding it a problem to be honest. When I'm driving in the car and I see people running, I just long to be able to do that again. I even get upset when friends talk about playing eighteen holes of golf, because I know I don't have the energy or the physique to do it anymore.

However, even the most depressing developments have something to teach you. I'm ashamed to admit that it has taken serious illness to make me appreciate how little outward characteristics should really matter. My family and friends have shown that they love me regardless of what I look like, and I have learned much more to look for the inner beauty in others.

The operation occupied most of my waking thoughts over the two-week lead up. I was desperate to get it over, unhappy about my readiness, frightened about the consequences and sad at leaving Nikki for the fortnight that I was expected to be in hospital. The hardest part of all was preparing my will and a letter for Nikki, should anything go wrong. It was the most difficult letter I have ever had to write, and left me feeling emotionally exhausted. Friends and family bolstered me in every way they could, but that strange lonely feeling I had experienced in my first hospital spell came back to me. When you are embarking on a journey you have to make alone, the more people there are to wave you off, the more lonely the impending journey appears.

It didn't work.

Mr Rees opened me up, went in, didn't like what he saw, and came straight out again, leaving a large new wound in my old scar and me back to square one. He said that I would have died if he had attempted the operation. The spread of tumours in the liver was too far gone for surgery to have any hope of success. That's it then. He had already told me that I would die if I didn't have the operation, that chemo alone wouldn't fix it.

I didn't know what to feel. I was just completely done in from sadness and exhaustion. Most difficult of all was what to say to people who asked me how it had gone. And how should I spend the short life remaining to me? A wild party every night or chug along as normal?

Mr Rees came and sat with me. He was so clearly upset that he had not been able to carry out the operation. I thanked him for trying and we wept together. I never would have believed this was something likely to happen, a top specialist crying with me, surgeons with the humanity and humility to show their feelings. It has changed my view of the medical profession. Afterwards we found a way to cheer ourselves up by talking about sport. He had been a top-class rugby player in his day and we shared some reminiscences about the Five Nations Championships. Before he left me, I told him that in six months time I would be back and he would be able to operate.

The truth really hit home the following day, and I cried almost from the moment I woke up. I was going to die soon and there was nothing anyone could do about it. The image of Nikki alone haunted me. My thoughts kept coming back to a conversation when she had envisaged the time I would be old and grey.

'I'll never be old and grey now. I've got to be able to talk to Nikki, to grieve with her and hug her.

God, let me wake up from this nightmare!'

My return to Hartswood Hospital was an emotional occasion. Staff had bought me flowers and a couple of them were in tears. It made me feel sad for them. Bernie Ribeiro came to see me and we cried together as well. He told me that I had up to six months left and that I had a choice whether or not to continue with the chemotherapy. On the one hand it would prolong my life a little, but the price would be greater discomfort during my remaining time. Some people opt for the higher quality of life and the chance to spend more of their last few months with their families.

Giving up the chemo was a valid option, reinforced in other conversations I had over the next few days. Why put yourself through all that grief and misery for perhaps an extra three months? But somehow I couldn't bring myself to consider giving up. I hadn't battled through the last few months to jack it in now. It felt as though I would be letting myself and others down, particularly Nikki. And anyway, I had already lived for longer than doctors expected the previous August. Who was to say that I wouldn't confound expectations again. The chemo had served me well during the autumn. I decided I wanted to hear what Neville Davidson had to say.

He came on the evening of my birthday. No false optimism, no skirting the realities of my position, but if I was ready to keep fighting it, he would go with me. He offered no guarantees about how long he could keep me going; only that he could treat me, and that if the tumours were responding, then I had a chance. It was what I wanted to hear. He left me feeling that we had to give it a try. I must make it. Even if I don't succeed, I must have tried to make it.

There was a fair bit of anger in me at this time. Anger at being opened up and left in a worse condition than before. Anger that my cancer had been allowed to progress to such an advanced stage before being detected. Why hadn't it been discovered during that year of appointments, tests and consultations? Captured earlier, my liver would have been operable and by now I would be well on the way to long-term remission. Puzzlement gave way to deep resentment. Closure of the surgical option had starkly presented me with the consequences of delayed diagnosis. Resentment has to land somewhere, and inevitably some of mine landed on the medical profession. However, if I focused on any individual doctor, the anger swiftly disappeared;

evaporated by their obvious distress and concern for me, together with the high standard of professional care they were providing. Even general undirected anger didn't last for long. Stewing over the twists of fate that have put you in this predicament achieves nothing. It also uses up valuable energy needed for fighting the wretched disease and getting on with your life.

The immediate aftermath of the operation felt like hitting the longest snake on the board. I needed some ladders to get myself back in the game, but there weren't too many around. Everything I had struggled to achieve in January and February was out of reach again. Physically whacked, it would be weeks before I would be able to swing a golf club. Six weeks away from work, that mountain had to be climbed again. My tumour levels, which had responded so well to seven months of chemotherapy, were a source of concern. Testing of carcinoembryonic antigen (CEA) levels in the blood can help to monitor the degree to which tumour cells are active in the body. In my case the reading had shot up from 500 to 3900 in the three weeks following the aborted operation. And, damn, I was about to lose my hair again.

The *Daily Mail* phoned to ask if it was true that the doctors could do nothing more for me, and then sent flowers! The *Mirror* and *Express* were on the next day. I wish I knew how they get hold of this stuff.

The tumour levels continued to go up and all the familiar accompaniments to my condition – sickness, pain, diarrhoea, exhaustion – rose to a depressing crescendo. I plunged myself once more into investigation of alternative therapies. I was persuaded to go to a couple of healing sessions, initially against my better judgement. Nikki came with me to the first. She watched while I went through all the holding and laying on of hands. Then in a small voice she asked for some healing herself. It released all the sadness bottled up in her, and she just cried and cried. She said that afterwards she felt a great weight had lifted, and for that reason alone I think it was worth doing. It was also a shared experience for us which was important.

At the second session a week later the healer claimed that a man in motorbike gear came to me and told me never to give up. Deep scepticism on my part, but just a hint of 'I wonder.' We had a friend years ago who died in a motorcycle accident.

Just when I was beginning to despair about my declining condition, things started to turn around. The tumour levels dropped by 25 per cent in a week and it felt as if my energy was flooding back. I managed nine holes on the golf course, kicked my diet into touch for a couple of days, and splashed out more than I have ever spent on anything with less than three bedrooms – a flash new Mercedes Roadster. 'What the hell. I've got cancer. I'm allowed to do this sort of thing. It's my pension.'

I booked Nikki and myself into a hotel in the New Forest over Easter. Great! After all the floods and rain of the previous weeks, the sun came out on Easter Monday and we went riding in the Forest. The weather seemed to mirror my state of mind, like emerging from a dark tunnel. It was wonderful to be able to get on a horse and to trot across sweet-smelling open ground.

The animal knew I didn't have the strength to control it, and took no notice of me at all, just went where it wanted to go. By the end of the week I might have been able to show it who was boss. Three days of lazing around, sampling the hotel pool and sauna and visiting holiday haunts from my childhood worked wonders on me. I came home almost ready to believe that I wasn't ill at all.

An old school friend, Sue Edwards, had suggested a trip to Lourdes. She felt that we should try all avenues, and although it wasn't something I would normally have considered, I was happy to go along with it. We booked a two-day trip, five of us: Sue and Deb – both school friends – my sister and Nikki. Out of freezing cold Stansted at the crack of dawn, and into even colder Lourdes. What a swizz! You'd have thought that by the end of April the Almighty might have arranged for a bit of sun to warm the foothills of the Pyrenees. Somewhat thoughtless of Him when all those poor souls are dowsing themselves in icy water in His name.

What did I expect? Well I guess a bit of solitude and serenity, a place not unlike a retreat, imbued with a spiritual atmosphere. What we encountered was something different, by turns tear-jerking, grossly commercial, and side-achingly hilarious. Never serene.

Our tour guide provided the first laugh. With his wild appearance and distinctly odd behaviour, he could have been taken for a particularly desperate pilgrim in search of relief from advanced dementia. Totally immersed in the Catholic experience, he whisked us from place to place, frequently to the wrong place, gibbering a non-stop incantation that seemed more like some personal act of devotion than a commentary for our benefit.

The area outside the grotto itself is like tourist traps the world over. Hundreds of people milling about, posing for group photos and wasting good videotape on interminable zooming and panning shots. There's a constant buzz of chatter which the authorities have obviously considered detrimental to the dignity of the place. So a man is employed to walk up and down with a microphone. Whenever he feels that the noise level has reached unacceptable proportions he intones a long *Shhh* into his microphone and it reverberates from a dozen PA speakers. Shuts them up for all of thirty seconds. Some job.

'What do you do for a living?'

'I stand outside a religious monument saying *Shhh* through a megaphone.'

I was shocked by the tacky commercialism of the place. Just outside the basilica area are hundreds of gift shops selling all manner of junk: Virgin Mary cigarette lighters, lamps, plastic snowstorms and tea towels; holy water containers in every conceivable size and shape, including – guess what – Our Lady shape. She's big business in Lourdes. Whatever else she may have done in the 150 years since she appeared to the miller's daughter, St Bernadette, in a crack in the rock, she has certainly managed to line the pockets of the town's entrepreneurs.

Don't misinterpret my retrospective cynicism. I went with an open mind and there were some bits of the trip I found intensely moving, like standing in the church with shafts of silver light descending from the highest windows upon hundreds of sick and disabled people below – but they were few and far between. We seemed to spend far more time convulsed with laughter. Not just a giggle here and there, but the helpless, desperate to suppress it variety that only comes in the company of people with whom you feel completely at ease and is rendered all the more deliciously painful by seeming to be vaguely naughty or irreverent.

There is something so crazy and brilliant about getting into that hysterical, tears rolling down the cheeks state. As a kid there was nothing I enjoyed more. I thought it had been a bad day if my friends and I hadn't rolled on the floor about something. I discovered the delight in making others laugh as well, became the class clown, and was completely addicted to practical jokes. I used to take a whistle down to break and on cold days I would blow it early and have the whole school lining up.

I'm less anarchic these days, but no less of a laughter addict. I'm set off at the most inappropriate moments. Worst are those times when you start to crease up at something which is meant to be serious. In television we call it corpsing, when you can no longer speak for trying to stifle a guffaw. I have never quite been out of control but I've been close. Names of sportsmen and women that have a double entendre are my speciality. I need to keep a firm grip on myself at some international events.

Everybody accepts that negative emotions like stress and worry make people ill, but we don't give enough attention to the therapeutic effects of a happy and positive disposition. That old saying 'Laughter is the best medicine' seems to have more than a grain of truth in it. I read recently about a chap called Norman Cousins who in 1964 was hospitalised with a crippling disease involving the disintegration of the connective tissue of the body. He decided to leave hospital, refuse any more pain-killing injections and to test a theory that laughter might bring about positive changes to his health. He hired a movie projector (no videos in those days) and watched every comic film he could get hold of. He found that ten minutes of laughter gave him two hours of pain-free sleep, and his health started to improve. Could lead to an interesting new prescription policy.

'Right, Helen. I'd like you to take one episode of *Friends* three times a day after meals, and half an hour of *Frasier* at bedtime.'

We decided to take part in the Lourdes evening candlelight procession and mass at the grotto. Five among hundreds, we bought the regulation candles with their paper weathershields and shuffled through the wind and sleet like extras from a Hollywood biblical epic. By the time we got to the grotto we were so cold that we had to huddle over our candles for warmth. The service was at its peak of solemnity when Ali's candle took pity on her hypothermic state and ignited its windshield. Result, hoots and squeals of laughter as we battled unsuccessfully to control what had become a portable bonfire. A nearby group of nuns emitted the sort of body language that would have made Spanish Inquisitors seem jovial and tolerant. We extinguished the towering inferno eventually by performing a passable display of Mexican fire dancing. All the stamping helped to get the circulation going.

Back at the hotel I shared with Deb my cynicism about the whole Lourdes shebang.

'I can't believe that this is going to make the slightest bit of difference. I've lost my faith in God.' As I spoke, the lights in our room went out.

Twenty seconds of darkness is just long enough to make a joke about yellow cards from the Almighty. With the light restored we checked that neither of us was leaning on the switch, and I continued with my diatribe. The lights went out again.

'Oh, come on now. That's not fair!'

At the baths alongside the grotto they immerse pilgrims, sick and hearty. You take up your position on long wooden benches either side of a corridor. Every couple of minutes the individual at the end of the bench is beckoned forward and everybody else shuffles up a place. When it's your turn to fall off the end of the bench, you're ushered into a changing area where there are helpers to assist you. It's a bizarre experience which involves stripping down to your bra, just your bra, and donning a thin robe.

My large, and obviously recent, operation scar prompted my helper to enquire about the nature of my illness. Somehow, telling a stranger about it in a place like that seemed to emphasise the enormity of my plight, and I was feeling distinctly shaky by the time my turn came to go through to the bath area. At this point the bra and robe are whipped away with sleight of hand that would do justice to an aspiring conjuror, and you are wound in a wet, white sheet; then seated in a long trough and gently but firmly dunked into the icy mountain spring water. It was as much an emotional shock as a physical one, and I was in tears when I came out. Needless to say, towelling this special water away is distinctly frowned upon, so it's a matter of tugging on your clothes over damp and clammy skin. Afterwards, when I wondered how many others had been in the same water as me, I was faintly repelled, but at the time it was a deeply moving experience.

6

Relative Harmony

THE Lourdes trip emphasised yet again just how brilliantly Nikki was coping with everything. She looked after me, carried my bags, mucked in with the rest of us and kept us smiling. When we arrived home she disappeared upstairs and re-emerged an hour later to present each of us with a hilarious, individually tailored certificate to mark the trip.

I have such respect for her. From the age of just fourteen she has coped with my illness and provided such mature strength and support that I sometimes have to pinch myself to remember that even now she is only just coming up to her sixteenth birthday. She has been a tower of strength at an age when so many kids have an attitude towards parents not dissimilar to that of Harry Enfield's Kevin.

We have always been close. I've worked since she was tiny, but I was luckier than many working mothers in that my job didn't fit the standard pattern and, despite long hours, I was able to juggle things so that I could spend time with her. I couldn't always manage it, of course. When you're working on a programme with a deadline looming, you can't just knock off and come back to it next day. You've got to carry on until it's right, and sometimes this meant me bombing out on family commitments. Mega-guilt.

I used to worry about the long absences when I was off covering international events. Would she be all right? What effect would the separation have on both of us? Talking to Nikki about it in recent years, it seems I need not have worried too much. She says she regarded my absence as the normal way of things, and has no recollection of being upset by it. The homecomings were quite wonderful. I remember coming back from the Seoul Olympics in 1988 to be greeted by a little five-year-old who ran the full length of the airport concourse to hug me.

Ironically, the most difficult separation was the Atlanta Olympics which required me to miss her thirteenth birthday. I felt bad about not being there on the day she entered her teens. The crew and I made an idiotic spoof video for her and arranged for her to receive it on her birthday. She had a great time with the people she was staying with, and the school arranged a picnic on the same day. All in all she probably had an even better time than normal, but with me the guilt levels were high.

My husband and I split up in 1991 and since then Nikki and I have rattled around together, a family of two. Nikki has an excellent relationship with her father and spends regular weekends and holidays with him. But inevitably she and I have become even closer, as we have shared the ups and downs of our lives together. Very similar in some ways, utterly different in others, we laugh at the same sort of things, share a love of sport and have the same horror about letting people down.

Our relationship is not entirely without its tensions. I'd be worried if it was. Like most teenagers she has a tendency to answer back, and doesn't give up easily. Arguments about trivialities can escalate into nuclear confrontations. The most frequent sources of disagreement lie with Nikki's disorganisation and my tendency to nag. She is laid back to the point of falling over and has a particular knack of losing things. Behind the cool façade, she's pretty conscientious, but I'm afraid I do get on at her when I feel she isn't doing herself justice. The last few months leading up to GCSEs have provided me with ample opportunity to practise my nagging parent routine and to be reminded of my need to chill out. What a hypocrite I am. As far as I can recall, preparation for my GCEs consisted of cramming my head with information over the last few days, and hoping it would stay there long enough for me to regurgitate it on to the exam paper.

It's unfortunate that Nikki's conscription to the laid-back ranks of British teens has corresponded with me becoming more picky than ever. My illness seems to have resulted in a heightened concern that everyday things around me should be just so. For much of the time I have been taking steroids, and they can have the effect of making you slightly aggressive. Every now and then I've flown off the handle, usually over something small. It happens rarely, but when it does it will make Nikki cry, and I end up absolutely hating myself.

These things are but slight hiccups in a relationship I treasure above all others. She looks after me, ministers to me, notices when I'm particularly tired, and plays her full part in any fun that's going. I am hugely proud of her.

We have done a lot more things together over the last couple of years – things that we might not have bothered with previously – shows, sporting events and so on. If I am invited to something and I'm up to it, we do it together. I hate the fact that I'm not well enough to take her easily on longer trips now. I would love to be able to pop off to places like Athens or Seville for a short break with her. She's a great tourist, loves the history of places, and is a lively holiday companion. But I have to recognise now that I'm unable to give her those sorts of experiences, and somebody else will have to do it for me.

I don't want to give the impression that Nikki and I are joined at the hip. She has her own life with her friends and does all the typical teenage things. I want her to have fun, and would trust her to know what she was doing in any social situation. What bothers me most is that the closeness of our relationship will come back and hit her in the face after I have gone. The vision of her alone in the aftermath of my death causes me much greater sadness than the prospect of my own departure. It's an almost unbearable thing for me to contemplate, and one over which I have wept at night many times.

I try to maintain a positive exterior for her sake. Occasionally I've let her see my bare emotions, which I think has been a mistake. Mostly I try not to let her know the full extent of how bad I feel. I know that she doesn't want to be reminded daily of the awfulness of the situation. She is no fool, she understands it perfectly, but it doesn't help to have it constantly pushed in her face. From time to time all the sadness she has bottled up wells out, and my heart just bleeds for her.

What of the future? I know she will cope, know she will make a success of her life. I ache to be a part of it, to see her through A levels and university, take pride in her achievements. But I know our time together is short and I cannot raise my gaze beyond the immediate path. I promised myself that I would see her through her GCSEs. At the time of writing that mission is virtually accomplished, and my next objective is to be there for the results. Beyond that? Well I'll wait and see. If I'm still at the wicket, there will certainly be another goal to set.

When I do go, I want there to be a good feeling, a shared knowledge that we have had something very special, the imprint of a beautiful relationship which will endure with her and ultimately triumph over the sadness and the hurt.

My brother and sister have also been very important throughout my illness. David spent a long time in hospital himself following a parachuting accident in his early twenties. He knows all about the trauma of it and has been very sensitive to my situation. His help has come in a quiet practical form, searching out information when I needed it, always there with advice and assistance but never pushing. With Ali I have shared some of the best and worst moments. We have laughed and wept together. She has always been very special to me, particularly since we have been adults, but the illness has, if anything, brought us even closer.

I was brought up the middle child of three, and when I say middle, I mean it precisely. David is two years nine months older than me, and Ali is two years nine months younger.

There's neatness for you, but then my parents were scientists. My father was an engineer who got out of the industry rat race and became a further education lecturer at Bath College. My mother was a biology teacher. David and I were adopted, while Ali followed along naturally. Ali is short for Alison, of course.

Until I was three we lived in Northampton, but there is nothing I can recall of that time. Bath is the childhood home I remember. We lived in a rambling and somewhat chaotic manor house at Batheaston about four miles along the A4 from Bath. In my childhood memory there were leaking ceilings and buckets around the place, but possibly that is an over-dramatisation. Rooms always seemed to be freezing in winter until we finally got central heating when I was in my teens.

We tended to be left very much to our own devices as far as entertainment was concerned, and there was huge scope to do our own thing around the house and garden. Indoors we played fiercely competitive board games for hours on end, nobody daring to leave the room during the game for fear of underhand activities while they were gone. There were endless opportunities for hide and seek in the numerous rooms. Once I managed to remain undiscovered for what seemed like hours by hiding in the base of a grandfather clock, a family heirloom which had been presented to my maternal grandfather by his employers on the occasion of his marriage. Using it as a hidey-hole was pretty sacrilegious and, although it may be just my imagination, I suspect that from then on it never kept such accurate time.

The enormous garden provided equal scope for adventure. There were thick bushes and trees down either side, ideal for climbing and constructing dens. Three players might seem inadequate for team games, but somehow we managed to play football, French cricket, hockey and a bunch of other stuff, too. I looked up to my brother and my goal was to prove myself as tough as him, whatever the sporting or physical challenge. I wasn't, of course. Not only was he faster and stronger, but I suspected that sometimes he made the rules up as he went along.

The desire to compete with him didn't go away. Even as young adults we couldn't resist a sporting challenge and on one occasion decided to have a one-mile race down at the local track. Right from the off it was clear he was going to run it from the front. He started to pull away from me but I stuck with him. After a couple of hundred yards he glanced round, saw I was still there and upped the pace. I hung on. Another hundred yards and he changed gear again, determined to shake me off. I dug deep to remain with him. With only a quarter of the distance gone we were both running flat out – no chance of either of us making it to the end. We collapsed before we had covered two laps out of four.

Ali provided me with early experience in management which I exploited to the full. I was the classic bossy elder sister. Still am, I'm afraid. Even now I can't resist venturing my opinions on how she should run her life. We would play and fight together at home, but school was a different matter. A different relationship was demanded there. Even in the junior school I recognised that it was seriously uncool to have your little sister hanging around you in the playground.

I used Ali as the willing subject in a variety of experiments.

93

I put chewing gum in her hair – it had to be cut out – and shaved the heads of her dolls to test whether the advertising claim 'hair that really grows' was accurate. On one occasion I cut her hair, too. Ali always wanted to have long hair, and hated the fact that the woman across the road, who normally cut our hair, was rather enthusiastic with the scissors. I convinced Ali that I could do it for her and not cut so much off. Of course, I made a terrible knife and fork job of it and as punishment we were both sent to bed. This turned out to be no punishment at all; we had a brilliant time fooling and laughing in the bedroom.

Not all experiments had such fun outcomes. There was the time when we tried to make a two-person human pyramid. Ali overbalanced while standing on my shoulders and suffered concussion for three days.

I was, and still am, more of a show-off than her and much readier to take centre stage. As teenagers we drifted apart somewhat, but our relationship flourished again when I was at college and she came down to visit me in my flat. We have remained very close ever since.

By no means all the things we did as children were carried out as a threesome. In that large house we were able to pursue our private interests. We were, and have remained, very independent and self-sufficient people. I relished the opportunity to be on my own at times, and I still do. There was almost nothing I enjoyed more than sitting in my room drawing and painting.

One of my most abiding childhood memories is of chickens. There were always plenty of them to be seen around the house and garden. Often it was my job to go and feed them at the crack of dawn. I hated the cold and was afraid of the dark, so winter mornings were sheer misery. The garden I knew like the back of my hand became a sinister place full of menacing shadows in the frost and gloom. Most of the chickens were speckled Grey Marans or Plymouth Rocks producing delicious big brown eggs, but we had a particularly nasty cockerel called Oscar Staggers who produced nothing but fear. He always seemed to be poised behind the chicken-house door waiting to leap out at me, hoping I would spill the feed right in front of him. I would stumble around attempting to gather the eggs as quickly as possible, while avoiding his vicious peck and sharp spurs. Bemused hens scuttled around my feet creating a further hazard. Using the fold of my jumper as an egg carrier was possibly not the best idea, and frequently there would be an accident. Broken egg down the inside of your wellingtons is an odd sensation. As a productivity incentive for some of the dopier chickens there were a few china eggs strategically placed to fool the stupid creatures into thinking they had already laid, and presumably to give them the incentive of pride in their accomplishment that they would be moved to attempt a repeat performance. In my bleary eyed state I was also frequently fooled, attempting to harvest these decoys with the rest.

We had bantams too – mini versions of standard breeds. They would wander the garden and come into the house as if they owned it, mingling in the kitchen with cats and humans. They fared better than their larger sisters in the parenthood stakes, hatching secret clutches of eggs in the undergrowth and emerging to delight us with families of fluffy chicks. Usually in each brood one would be struggling, and our standard procedure was to bring it into the house and put it in a shoe-box on the Aga cooker. I'm talking about the warm part, not the oven – that would come much later. A teaspoon of brandy and warm milk never seemed to fail, and within hours the lucky chick would back with its siblings, nursing nothing more than a hangover.

We were sometimes sent to a very special auntie when my parents had had enough. Auntie Jimmy, as she was nicknamed – my primary school teacher never could figure out the relationship – also kept hens and when I was very small she used to tell magical stories about them. When not weaving her stories, this aunt was a mine of information on everything under the sun. The stories centred on adventures that the chickens got up to once the chicken house had been closed up for the night. The chief character and unchallenged leader of the coop was one Black Leghorn who was the proud owner of a Rolls-Royce in which the hens would embark on all manner of adventures. Instead of leather seats the Rolls had perches and Black Leghorn had a capacity for ostentatious living which would have rivalled Elton John. Auntie Jimmy fired my tender imagination into orbit and I adored her.

As a young adult with an interest in art, I had the notion of recapturing these stories in the form of a book which I would illustrate, but I never quite got around to it. Other priorities intervened. Interestingly, the only book I ever got around to illustrating was a version of Rapunzel. Shortly after I was married, when we were particularly hard up, I sold it at an arts and crafts fair for twelve quid. One of those things you regret afterwards. Wonder where it is now?

David provided me with the nickname 'Buckit' which stayed with me into adulthood. It came from nothing more than a photo of me as a pre-school child with a bucket on my head, but it stuck right through school and college (the name that is, not the bucket). I can't blame anybody but myself for the perpetuation of my nickname. I was the one who passed it on from one phase of my life to the next. Arriving home at the end of her first day in senior school, Deb Baker, soon to be my friend, announced to her mother, 'There's a new girl in the class, and her name's Buckit.' It's a seriously unflattering name when you think about it, but it was a bit different and I liked that. Incidentally, if you are wondering whether my spelling is at fault here, let me reassure you. I simply preferred it spelt that way. I'm still Buckit or Buck to my sister and some close friends. At work I'm Rollas. Sometimes I wonder why I ever bothered with a first name.

I can't remember exactly when I learned I was adopted. I think I was about nine or ten. It came up by accident when for some reason our birth certificates were needed. But it wasn't something we were encouraged to discuss. With my Mediterranean appearance, I didn't physically resemble other members of my family and I recall speculating about that at some stage. Whether the knowledge of my adoption has had any bearing on the way I have approached life, I really can't say. I like to think not, but then none of us really knows what drives our unconscious. Certainly awareness that we were not biologically related never made any difference to the love and regard I had for my sister and brother.

It's my understanding that neither of my birth parents was

British. They happened to be living here at the time of my birth. So you could say that I was adopted by the country as well as by my mum and dad. Ironic isn't it, that I've spent a career rooting for British sport when I don't have a drop of British blood in me?

7

May to October 1998

AFTER a week which had included Easter in the New Forest and the trip to Lourdes I felt great. Life was so good I could almost convince myself that I wasn't ill. But I was quickly back on my personal roller coaster. The news of Linda McCartney's death hit me hard. There were so many things that struck a chord with my own situation. Her cancer had started in the breast but had spread to the liver like mine. And the reports said once that has happened there's nothing that can be done. They also described how uncharacteristically tired she was – just couldn't get up. I was thinking, 'I feel like that most of the time.' I would never wake naturally, always needed to be woken. But it was such a shock because I had been thinking how wonderful she looked in the recent pictures at Stella's fashion show in Paris. It really frightened me. I didn't sleep at all the night I heard the news. When I went in for chemo the next day, I heard that the breast care nurse had received dozens of calls from frightened women who wondered what hope there was for them if all the money and all the help in the world couldn't get her through it.

My tumour levels which had taken such a dramatic dip started to yo-yo again, and my hair was falling out again as the result of a new round of campto treatment. All very depressing. I began to fret about wasting time. With a limited ration of life remaining to me I needed to be doing things, but I didn't always feel well enough. At least there was a return to work in the offing. Sadly, it would be accompanied by the dreaded wig.

As before, it was a Saturday evening which marked my return. Once I was in the studio and had got my head around the new computer, it felt as if I had never been away. There was a longer than normal gap between the early and the late bulletins because of the Eurovision Song Contest and we went out for an Indian meal during the break. I dilly dallied for too long on my return thinking that the late bully was 11.15 rather than 11.00 and only just made it on air – no make-up and mouth raw from the curry. But it went well, and it was great to be there with Peter Sissons. 'Hope I'm back now.'

A suggestion came up that I might like to do a programme which was a sort of personal diary during the World Cup, a combination of my life and my thoughts on the football. I felt uneasy about it.

'By the time it goes out people will have had enough of the World Cup.'

'Umm, you're right, perhaps it's not such a good idea.'

But then I was chatting to Peter Salmon, the Controller of Programmes, and I told him that if I was going to do anything which touched on my life, I would want to be sure that it didn't trivialise the health issues or my situation. He said he was pleased by that because he would much prefer to do a proper programme on me and how the cancer was affecting my life. From that conversation sprang the QED programme *Hope for Helen*. As the discussion and planning for it started to unfold, I became increasingly committed to making it a success. I felt that it needed to be of use to other cancer sufferers – some of the people who had been writing to me over the months – to ask and answer some of their questions. A bloke called Michael Houldey was earmarked as the producer/director. I had not come across him before, but was pleased to learn that he had directed the series of documentaries on the Alder Hey Children's Hospital. 'Should be good,' I thought. He turned out to be absolutely brilliant – sensitive and instinctive, no jarring notes at all.

We started filming in mid-June. The first session was at the hospital during one of my chemo sessions and while I had a scan. The film crew was never more than four, including the director, which made it a lot less intrusive than I might have expected. I made sure that nurses who had been particularly special to me over the months were on duty for this session, and they were real stars – Jackie and Lynne. It always amazes me when I see how people who have never been in front of a camera before blossom quite naturally and behave like complete pros. The crew filmed us watching the England v Tunisia match, which fortunately England won 2:0.

The next day I went to the Second Test at Lord's with the film crew in tow. I grumpily registered that the place seemed to be full of old men with fat bellies, red noses and snobby accents. I was soon ashamed of my rush to stereotype. So many people came up to me saying how lovely it was to see me looking so well. I was really touched. It's so easy to dismiss people before they have had a chance to show what they are about.

I spent a lot of time awake at night thinking about the documentary. I decided it had to speak to people who had just been diagnosed with cancer that day. I wanted to do something which would help them not to be afraid. It was very important that the film should get across the way in which each of us is unique and responds in different ways. There's no reason for anyone to feel that the progress of their illness is inevitable. That's what I'm hanging on to.

I was pleased to find that Michael shared the same sort of objectives and was intent on capturing a natural and truthful account of my life with cancer. We agreed that we would take life as it came and not allow the technical and programme-making process to get in the way of telling the story. This meant, as far as humanly possible, avoiding the repeat takes which normally bedevil filming. It was also important for me to step aside completely from my professional persona. I must not be a television presenter presenting myself, but simply what I was – a person with cancer and a teenaged daughter.

Oddly, the one time during the making of the film when I found the cameras a real intrusion was when they filmed me at work. Otherwise it was pretty easy to deal with. In fact, with the sessions at hospital, being able to talk to the crew about the treatments I was undergoing helped me deal with the boredom and the discomfort. The longest day of filming was a trip to a World Cup game in Lens – England v Colombia. Nikki, who had never had a camera near her, suddenly had one up her nostrils all day. She reacted very naturally, which thrilled me, and she didn't pretend to be anything that she wasn't. Quite honestly, she was far more natural than I was. Now that's an admission from somebody who makes her living in front of a camera.

It was a pretty hefty day. Up at 6.30 to catch the 9.27 Eurostar from Ashford and filmed on the way to Lille. Then off to Lens to meet up with the mob from the Beeb. It was great; everybody made us feel so special. Of course, it wasn't totally spontaneous. There was somebody from *Grandstand* running around ahead of us to make sure that we would be in the right place at the right time with the cameras rolling, to capture those chance encounters with Gary Lineker, Rob Bonnet and the rest. We had lunch with John Motson and Trevor Brooking. Motty brought his match notes and tables for Nikki, and after the game he gave me the notes to auction for the HEAL cancer charity. Then it was off to the stadium with our painted faces and Nikki's red and white hair. I didn't wear my wig. First time on television and I was a bit uneasy about it. But I knew it was the right thing to do.

The match was great. England won 2:0 and could have had 5. Beckham and Anderton scored two cracking goals which sent us into quite genuine raptures. No playing to the cameras needed at all. Fortunately the cameras weren't with us the following week when England went down to Argentina 4:3 on penalties. There was a bit of weeping around the television set that night.

Given my involvement with television and pretty strong views about what I wanted the film to do, there was potential for a clash with the director. But I'm pleased to say that harmony was the order of the day. I put in my five pennyworth and he listened and responded. Michael approached others featured in the film directly – the doctors, therapists and colleagues – and they talked about my treatment and attitudes. I felt no worries about that. They could just be honest and say what was going on.

Nikki and I had a holiday booked in Polzeath at the beginning of July and planned to meet up with my brother and family who were also holidaying there. As ever, the lead up wasn't great. I worked the previous evening and got quite angry about a couple of glitches. The first was a problem with timings, but the second was much more irritating. I gave out wrong information because somebody had been too lazy to check the up-to-date position. I hate that.

It's a bloody long way to Cornwall. Somehow I always forget how far. We stayed with Ali overnight in Bristol on the way. Stupidly, we watched a TV drama about a woman with cancer. She had a daughter and was anxious not to die doolally and yellow like her mother had. Loads of it hit home, very upsetting, and we wished we hadn't turned it on. When you see something like that, so germane to your own situation, it makes you wonder how many other things broadcast each day are driving a cold wedge into some viewers.

The hotel was fantastic, brilliant view over the estuary to Rock. And the food was healthy – makes a change. Nikki and I had a very special morning walking over the rocks and loving just being by the sea. I had a dream the first night there that Nikki and I were trying to find our way in the dark and fog. We were picking our way over every inch of ground and it seemed to go on forever.

My dreams at this time had become exceptionally vivid, and in amongst familiar themes were references to my current state of health and mind. Some of them stayed with me after I had woken up. One night I dreamt I was playing golf on a course made of chocolate bars. I woke up instantly, aware of my craving, guilty about the frailty of my recent resolve to maintain a chocolate-free existence and convinced that very shortly I would succumb to the temptation yet again. Is this what drug addicts go through? I know that it's doing me harm and here I am dreaming about the stuff. On another occasion I dreamt I was in a prisoner of war camp. I had to stand up in front of thousands of people and make a speech. As I got up on the podium I realised I had nothing written, nothing to say. It was a new twist on an old theme. I have this recurrent dream about being on air with nothing prepared. In a third nocturnal adventure I was climbing a rockface to join my school classmates who were at the top. I was a schoolgirl, but I was grown up. The people climbing up behind me were all in suits. There were pitons embedded in the rock to provide holds, and as I climbed, petrified, one broke and I was plunged back down. I said, 'I haven't got the will power to try again. I just can't do it all over again.'

I wondered whether the dream thing was anything to do with my chemo regime. Certainly it had led to some other odd effects with my mind. Whenever I was receiving the dreaded campto I felt hugely creative, full of ideas and wanting to write and paint. Sadly however, whatever it might be doing for my creativity, it didn't seem to be helping very much with the tumours. The levels stayed stubbornly high, despite every effort to zap them. Dr Davidson decided that I must have become resistant to campto and proposed to replace it with another concoction called oxaliplatin which would be administered with the old favourite 5FU every two weeks. It seemed to have the desired effect, the levels dropped 400 points in a week. A couple of weeks later I was feeling dim and forgetful. Could that be down to the chemo as well, or was I just blaming the chemo for what is my normal state?

Chemotherapy was far from being the only invasion of my body by dubious chemicals. I was heavily reliant on pain patches and was finding it very hard to sleep without temazepam. 'I'm getting addicted to the stuff, must try to wean myself off it.' Easier said than done – some nights I didn't sleep even after taking it, lying there, sweats, cramps, miserable. My veins were starting to protest from all the injections I had been given. It was becoming increasingly difficult to find a suitable spot on my pincushion arms, and Whoa! here's a new thing – pins and needles in my hands, feet and throat every time I touch something cold. For all that, the doctors remained decidedly upbeat. With the number of tumours in my liver, it was amazing that I was still standing. An MRI scan confirmed what they were saying. There appeared to be hundreds of tumours on the screen. I was very scared during the scan this time. Cried and felt as if I was going into my coffin. The QED team were there during the two and a half hours it took, but I hardly noticed them.

The full impact of my lack of improvement hit me when I

saw the scan results. I felt an enormous sense of disappointment. Being the eternal optimist I am, I had hoped that some of the little tumours would have gone, and that there would be clear patches in the liver. But no, everything was much the same as before. I could recognise the large tumours instantly and the small ones seemed to fill the rest of the liver. It was hugely depressing.

I've worked so hard – diet, Chinese medicine, exercise and rigid adherence to my medical regime. None of it has worked, and my tumour levels are up again.

It's all very well for the doctors to express surprise and delight over the fact that I have survived for so long, but I don't just want to be an unusually long-running survivor. I want to be a survivor full stop. I want to be the one who makes them reassess the standard prognosis for patients with advanced liver cancer. It may seem a bit selfish of me, but nothing else is quite good enough.

I was devastated to learn that my friend Tracy Harte who was fighting with me against this shitty disease had died. Tracy, who bounced into my hospital room almost a year previously, announced that it had been her room, gave me a teddy bear and said, 'Come on, kiddo, we can beat it.' Tracy who had walloped golf balls like a pro by comparison with my feeble taps. I couldn't believe it. And at just thirty-five. Far too young. I felt terrible that I hadn't known she was in hospital for the last couple of weeks before her death. I should have seen her to give the support she gave me. Sorry Trace.

Death seemed well and truly on the agenda at this time. Another friend died within days, and I was conscious of the first anniversary of my own diagnosis. Easily the most eventful year of my life. My world had been changed beyond recognition – 70 mph to 10 mph with flat tyres. I ate a bar of organic chocolate to celebrate the year. Felt fat and headachy afterwards. Trevor Brooking, bless him, remembered the date of my diagnosis and phoned to cheer me up.

That night I woke around 3 a.m. with a tremendous pain around my liver and the top of my rib cage. I was sick and began to worry that my liver was failing. Managed to get downstairs for some painkillers which helped a lot, but I was more frightened than I'd been for a long time. Sadly, the next day I had to stay in bed and dipped out of a planned get-together with my three college friends.

Hard on the heels of my own anniversary came all the tributes to Princess Diana one year on. That brought it flooding back again – how ill I was then, how much pain there had been since. Tracy was constantly in my thoughts and the image of Nikki alone kept returning to me.

I'm on borrowed time here.

On the morning of 30th August the television came on by itself. Yes, honestly! One of the breakfast items was a recording of Roy Castle, with his wonderful wife, talking about making the most of his last few months. His wonderful sunny disposition inspired me. If he could rise above it, so can I.

For the last week of the school holidays, Nikki and I grabbed a further few days in Cornwall. This time we took the train rather than make the interminable drive, but it was so crowded I began to regret it. We got to Truro only to find that I'd left my driving licence at home so couldn't hire the car I had booked until the hire company had contacted DVLC. Too late to phone them that day. Aargh! Taxi to Falmouth and then back again the following morning to pick up the hire car. John Prescott take note – it's going to take one hell of a lot to wean us away from the cosy convenience of our cars. We divided our time between Falmouth, St Ives and Polzeath. Beaches, friends, good food, mooching. Nikki swam in the icy sea but I had to decline. Pins and needles as soon as I put my feet in the water. We gave the QED film crew half a day and they filmed us on the beach at Polzeath, plus some moody shots of us walking and sitting on the headland with the sun dipping into a glorious surfer's sea.

I'm writing this several months after the QED film went out, but just a couple of weeks ago a woman from Plymouth wrote to me about the shot I've just mentioned – Nikki and me walking and sitting on the headland. She said that a few years ago her son, a keen surfer, was killed in a motorcycle accident. She was watching the QED film and to her amazement saw Nikki and me sitting on the bench which she and her husband had donated to the memory of their son. Connections come about in the oddest ways, don't they? It was such a deeply moving letter.

Now how can a kitten make such a difference to your life? A beautiful scrawny little thing given to me by one of the nurses who said we needed something else to love around the house. She was right. It cheered up both of us instantly. After kicking around several rather pretentious Latin names, we lighted on the name Henna for our new companion.

I was interested to discover that there is a school of thought known as pet therapy which asserts that animal ownership can make a genuine improvement to your health. There is evidence that suggests benefits in the form of reduced anxiety, greater relaxation, more positive attitude, lower blood pressure and better general well-being. Apparently, pet therapy is big in the USA. There are pet therapists who visit nursing homes, hospices and even prisons with dogs in tow. The claim is that it works in a similar way to having supportive human beings around us, but pets have the advantage of a form of unconditional love which is sometimes difficult for humans to match.

Well, I wouldn't go quite that far. Henna is wonderful to have around. I love her and she definitely makes me feel better, but when it comes to comparing her with my family and friends, sorry pussy, you're not quite up there. But then I am very lucky in the human support I've had. In other circumstances I can imagine that a pet might be a reason to go on living.

Dr Willoughby called by and among other things told me I had got fat. He didn't mean it rudely; a few months previously it was my lack of weight that was causing concern. But he hit a raw nerve, I *was* getting fat. He thought it was the chemo. I thought it was the muesli biscuits. I was desperate to exercise. Keith Morton, the trainer who had got me so fit in the mid-nineties, had devised an exercise programme for me, and I had been trying to get regular swimming and golf sessions in. Usually, though, they left me exhausted. I only had a limited amount of energy each day. Use it up on exercise and there's none left for anything else. Then, out of the blue would come a day when I was feeling great, whacking golf balls straight and hard, ready for anything. Sadly, these days weren't coming round often enough, and I consoled myself with chocolate.

I was approached to do a piece for a programme called *Holiday Heaven*, a personal view of a favourite holiday destination. It could be anywhere I chose. I kicked around a number of possibilities but eventually settled on Polzeath. The QED producer Michael Houldey would have rather I had chosen somewhere else because we had already featured Polzeath in that film, but I was sure that the purpose and treatment of the two films would be very different. I was excited about the idea of doing it, something different, and it helped mollify my annoyance at being overlooked for the World Cup athletics, the thing I think I do best.

By now you may be vaguely interested in why this particular bit of North Cornwall is so important to me. Well, it goes back to childhood of course. As a family we used to holiday in various places: the New Forest, Wales and the West Country, but North Cornwall was always my favourite. There is something magical about the place which keeps me coming back again and again.

My family seemed to make a specialism of owning thoroughly unreliable cars. The one I remember best was a Ford Zephyr, which invariably broke down whenever we set off on holiday. There would be interminable roadside delays waiting for the AA before we were able to resume our journey. In truth they were probably not as long as my memory paints them, but one hour can seem like ten to a small child desperate to get to the seaside.

Our holiday accommodation was a big old orange canvas tent which also seemed to take an age to erect. Tiger the cat, who accompanied us on all our holidays, would delight in scrabbling up the space between tent and fly sheet, and sliding back down again. Strangely, the cat didn't seem to be terribly put out by the sudden change of location. She did take the odd walkabout though, and on one or two occasions somebody had to be left behind when we were due to depart, in order to wait for her to return.

I learned to play cricket on the beach, and loved to run from point to point along the shoreline splashing through the thin fringing wavelets. We would attempt to surf, none too successfully, using a plank of wood as a body board. Our approach to the sun would have latter day parents throwing up their hands in horror. Sun block, what's that? The only factor you heard of in those days was Max Factor. Of course, we didn't always get burnt. Sun was often at a premium. On every holiday, at least one day seemed to be spent in the laundrette reclaiming our garments from the effects of a West Country downpour.

The final piece of filming for the QED programme was at a charity 'do' in support of the HEAL cancer charity. Neville Davidson, my oncologist, is the chairman of HEAL and I had acquired various pieces of sports memorabilia which were to be auctioned during the evening. Jim Davidson the comedian (no relation to Neville) had agreed to compere the evening and I sat next to him. I hadn't met him before and I have to say I was a little uncertain about what to expect. He turned out to be the most excellent company: charming, witty and amusing, not at all like his boorish press image. He turned the charity auction into a virtual cabaret and really drew everyone into the spirit of it. I changed my view of him entirely. The sporting souvenirs up for auction, had been mainly due to the efforts of my good friend Peter Allden, the producer of *Sport on Friday*. He had badgered and ferreted to get hold of some terrific items. There was a football signed by the whole England World Cup squad which raised £3000, and a number of other items fetched really good prices. To complete the good vibes around the event, there were stacks of my friends present. Altogether an uplifting experience.

I had been hoping that I could lay off the chemo for a while. The constant hits were so exhausting. But the tumour levels kept bobbing up again. Dr Davidson said he wanted to have one more go with oxaliplatin, then a four-week break, followed by a different regime. I became convinced that I was going to lose my hair for the third time. I didn't, as it happened, but the prospect of continuing for much longer with the wretched wig depressed me terribly. Very shortly the viewing public would see my bald head in the QED film. After that, I desperately wanted to be able to go on air with my own short, natural hair.

Cornwall again, three days this time for the *Holiday Heaven* film. What constitutes my ideal holiday in my ideal place? Well, first it was across to Padstow for a meal at Rick Stein's restaurant. Very good and very expensive – thank you BBC. The next morning golf at the St Enedoc golf course – I was pretty crummy, if not utterly embarrassing – and then to Padstow again where they filmed me painting by the harbour. I love to be able to paint on holiday. It's one of the great delights of my life for which there's just not enough time in the normal frenetic week. The third day was delightful. We filmed on the edge of the surf, ate at Finns Café – brilliant fresh fish followed by chocolate mousse – chatted to Pete and Jane at Surf's Up surfing school and finished off with the obligatory shot of me on Pentire Point soaking up a majestic evening. No drugs, pain patches or alternative therapies can give me the same benefits I get from feasting on my favourite view. Try it! View therapy – it can make you feel just great to be alive. What's more, the BBC were paying for it.

The whole thing was pretty laid back. Just a two-man film crew to contend with. Simon, the producer, director, cameraman, likes to film everything three times, but he's so nice that I was prepared to forgive him. Back to London feeling as if I'd had a proper holiday and I immediately ran into one of those self-opinionated cab drivers who seem to spend their time contriving to be at the front of the rank just as my turn comes around. This one spent the journey from Paddington to Liverpool Street justifying at length the reasons why he couldn't support England. It boiled down to the fact that he supported Chelsea. I should have just let him prattle on, but I argued with him and began to take his failure to see sense personally. He was probably just winding me up for the sake of it. Certainly succeeded – my mood was a deal blacker when I got out of his cab.

The QED film was finally ready and I was invited to view it. A very strange experience. I tried to sit back and look at it objectively as a piece of television rather than a film about me. Not easy to do, but I thought it was excellent. It made me laugh and cry, and I was so grateful that the central message had come across. The one thing I wanted other cancer patients to take away from the programme was: don't fear cancer – tackle it head on and try and make something of your life.

Publicity shot for the 21st European Swimming
Championships, 1993.

Seoul 1988, working for ITV – my first Olympics. Here's Daley Thompson, wh
was coached by my good friend Frank Dick, competing in the decathlon.

Harry Carpenter takes it on the chin. Commonwealth Games, Auckland 1990.

The 1990 Commonwealth Games – with fellow presenters (*left to right*) Steve Rider, Des Lynam, and Peter Jones.

This is one they took before the stress of covering Wimbledon 1990.

My first *Grandstand*, May 1990 – poor picture quality could be because it's a video still, or maybe just me shaking with fright.

And this is how it looks from where I sit. The *Sport on Friday* studio.

The 1996 Atlanta Olympics. Sensationally presented, but hot, exhausting and soulless.

Left: Noel Thatcher on his way to victory in the Atlanta Paralympics 10,000 metres.

Below: Interviewing Noel the day after the race.

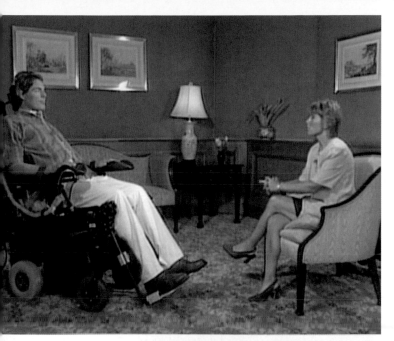

Above: With Christopher Reeve – the most memorable interview of my career.

Right: Tanni Grey powering home in the 400 metres at the Barcelona Paralympics, 1992.

At the Des Lynam Celebrity Golf Day, Royal Mid-Surrey, September 1996.
(*Inset*) The Jimmy Hill Celebrity Golf Day, May 1996 (it's not Jimmy in the suit!).

Looking at the finished product I reflected on the process of making it. Some things had been difficult to talk about, particularly those times when things had gone wrong medically, but on the whole I had enjoyed it. I felt there had been an important reason for doing it, and that it had worked out well. The film actually helped me with the illness in a stepping stones sort of way. I hadn't got a lot on work-wise during the main period of filming, so it gave a bit of extra structure to my weekly routine. I didn't do anything different, but it was a case of, 'Oh, I'm in hospital this week and Michael is going to be there with the tape.' Those hospital visits are not always the most pleasant of experiences and sometimes they can be made much better by having people to think about other than yourself. I'd enjoyed talking to them, explaining what was happening. The film actually brought together both sides of my life.

Between the first private showing and the broadcast was the pre-publicity. Television trailers and various articles began to surface. All sorts of appearance requests came my way. There is a fine line between helping people and self-publicity, and I began to feel dangerously close to stepping over it. The producer was asked to cut five minutes off the running time, and I worried that a recent dream, in which the programme was completely changed, might come true.

I could barely watch the broadcast. I was staying with old friends, we got an Indian take-away and then settled down to watch. But I was like a cat on hot bricks, so anxious about how it would come over. It's a big thing to appear on the telly giving your own views on a subject as important and technical as cancer, totally different from presenting and reporting on events and developments in your own field of expertise. I didn't want to come across as somebody who thought she had all the answers, and I was really worried that people might say, 'Well, what the hell does she know?' and be quite justified in saying it. In fact, I don't remember ever getting a letter indicating that at all.

The response was amazing. It still is. I still get letters saying, 'I have been meaning to write to you since last October,' or, 'I've been lent the film by a friend.' I was very pleased with the reaction because it's always a risk to do something like that. I didn't think it would be as big as it was. I thought it might have a profound effect on people who had the illness, but I didn't think for one minute that so many people would be affected by it and would be bothered to pick up a pen and write to me.

I was anxious about the reaction of those around me too, but I needn't have worried. My mother phoned after the programme to tell me how good she thought it was. She isn't a person given to lavish expressions of feelings and so her call meant a lot to me. The reactions of colleagues were quite extraordinary. Many said how moved they were, and felt I had done the right thing by making it. I think it also helped with some colleagues who hadn't previously realised quite how ill I was. I needed to get the message across that I could no longer jump in and out of boats or cope with physically demanding assignments any more. The programme did that for me.

When I look back upon it almost nine months on, I realise how much has changed in my health and attitudes over that time. If the film were to be made now, I think it would be a very different one. I would probably be more cynical about the alternative medicines, and there might be more black humour in it. I would also be open about the fact that I am closer to dying now and that I fear for Nikki more. There was a suggestion that we might make a follow up, but that hasn't got off the ground. In many ways this book is the follow up.

8

Good Eggs

'A true friend is someone who thinks you are a good
egg even though he knows you are slightly cracked.'

BERNARD MELTZER

WHERE would I be without my friends? I really would
never have got this far. Their unconditional love and
support has carried me through when things looked bleak. The
therapeutic effect of fun times and laughter has strengthened
me and helped me to deal with setbacks and disappointments.
They've been just great.

You know how it is with friends in normal times. You're
busy with your separate lives, seldom meeting up as often as
you would really like because of work or home commitments.
Always a matter of good intentions, a snatched phone call, the
odd note. 'We must get together. I'll give you a call in the next
couple of weeks and we'll arrange something.' Then suddenly
it's Christmas and you realise with a shock as you write your
cards that months have gone by since you last saw them. So you
leap for the phone or scribble on the card: 'Must get together
soon. I'll phone you.'

And, of course, they are busy writing exactly the same thing on your card.

Well, one of the few positive things about this illness is that good intentions are realised and I do see the people I love much more frequently. Whereas previously I might have seen my old friends two or three times a year, now it will be every three or four weeks, and I'll talk to them regularly on the phone in between. They are people with jobs and families who have put themselves out to a quite remarkable degree, there when I need them, sensitive to the situation. They have had to adjust to life with the disease as I have. It has probably made us all re-evaluate our lives. I don't think any of us take anything for granted anymore.

You could map my life by my friends. Like the rings in a tree trunk each group marks a different phase. It's a source of great pleasure to me that I haven't lost touch with many along the way. People who were important to me as a child and teenager are still with me now.

Deb and I met at the age of eleven. I had just arrived at Bath High, disgruntled that my parents had refused to let me go to Keynsham Grammar where all my primary school friends were going. She had come through from the junior branch of the school, so was not quite as cast adrift as I, but her best buddy had just gone off to a private school, so she too needed a new friend. We recognised each other as kindred spirits – same rebellious streak, same crazy sense of humour. My memory suggests that she led me on to the point where I got into trouble, but she claims it was the other way round, and that I was the one who couldn't resist taking the joke a bit too far. Certainly, there were times when I milked every last laugh out of a situation, but it was the appreciative audience in the form of Deb, Sue and my other classmates what made me do it. God's truth, yer honour!

We had a music teacher, Mrs Dewey, who had what I might call an idiosyncratic way of conducting whenever we had to do any singing. Taking her off was the easiest thing in the world, and guaranteed to get a laugh if you could do it without her seeing you. Such was my desire that everyone in the class should benefit from my performance, she caught me at it. She was very very angry, and I was made to stand in the corner. The lesson started up again, but as soon as her back was turned, I was unable to resist providing an encore. Bum notes and muffled snorts from the assembled warblers alerted her to the fact that something was taking place behind her back. Whoops! Caught again. This time with dire threats ringing in my ears I was exiled to the corridor from where I could create no further havoc. That's what you think, Mrs Dewey. As soon as the music started up again, I quietly opened the door, slid an arm around it, and treated the class to a final disembodied impersonation, before drawing myself back into the corridor, almost collapsing with mirth as I imagined the reaction to my antics. 'Tee hee! Didn't catch me that time, Mrs D.'

This was pretty typical stuff, but there was another occasion when I went too far and wound up with more than a spell in the corridor. It had snowed. There's something about snow on a school-day that turns even the most docile children into hyperactive monsters. Half the class hadn't made it in and neither had one of our teachers, so a student teacher was pressed into action at short notice. Snow and a student teacher – lethal combination. Faced with a class of jumping beans she made a valiant effort, but we were intent on having some fun at her expense. Somebody in the class asked her what rape meant – a sure-fire way to embarrass an insecure teacher. The poor thing became terribly flustered and wouldn't tell us. So I got the dictionary out, stood up and read the definition to the class. It got back to the headmistress and I was sent home and told I was suspended until further notice. A pretty OTT reaction on the part of the school, you may think, but remember this was a girl's high school thirty years ago.

I walked home the three or four miles in the snow. When I got there, I found that my parents had already been informed. They were sitting there absolutely livid. I was sent to my room and not allowed to go out for God knows how long. I went back to school on a promise that I would behave myself. Perhaps I did improve a bit, but if we didn't have hysterics at least once a day, I felt it was a failed day. I was always in detention and on one occasion I was party to the whole class being given detention. Two of us succeeded in locking the classroom door by fiddling in the lock with a piece of wire. I should point out that the whole class was inside the room at the time, and the French teacher was due to arrive to take the lesson. She appeared outside the room, found she couldn't get in and proceeded to work herself up into a blind fury. She shouted instructions at us through the door, 'Get your books out. Do exercise three on page sixty-two.' No way could we comply. We were so creased up by the sight of her livid face up against the glass, it was as much as we could do to remain sitting on our chairs. Eventually the caretaker had to come and break the lock. Result, shared detention and shared repair bill.

But I shared good fortune as well as bad. Like the time when I found the exam papers for the following week's English exam. I didn't keep them to myself, but made sure that everyone in the class had a copy. We all did absolutely brilliantly. I found it such a joke. For all my naughtiness, I got on pretty well with the teachers. I wasn't surly or unco-operative. From my own fairly brief teaching career, I can say that those are the traits that most get up teachers' noses. At least enthusiastic mischief brightens up the lesson.

After our O levels, Deb and I were allowed our first independent holiday. I use the word 'holiday' loosely. It was actually a pea-picking expedition to Lincolnshire. My father drove us up there and we camped on land belonging to some people my parents knew, so not exactly complete independence, but for two sixteen-year-olds it felt like freedom. Sadly, liberty was not accompanied by wealth. It was payment by results, and the results of our efforts were distinctly unimpressive. The most we managed to earn in a day was £1 each. Everyone else seemed to be able to do it so much faster. We tried bulb-cleaning, but without any greater success.

A fellow worker took pity on us and invited us to her house for a meal. She was a middle-aged woman with a strapping son who seized his opportunity to pull a couple of birds on home turf. He and his mates took us to the pub, and though the evening was harmless to the point of not even registering on the Richter scale, somewhere along the way I wound up with that great teenage emblem – the purple lovebite.

Now this was a matter of very serious concern. There was absolutely no way I could return home with my neck adorned in this fashion. I had no doubt that apoplexy would understate the parental reaction. I tried covering it with make-up. Hopeless. Pulling my collar up and hunching my shoulders didn't work either. The thing peeped cheekily over the top, visible from twenty paces. For the rest of the holiday, I anxiously monitored its progress through the colour card – purple to brown to yellow to grey – constantly trying to estimate whether it would fade in time.

Our pub escorts turned up at our tent the following evening, hoping for another bite at the cherry, as it were. But I wasn't interested any more. To avoid another night at the pub, I unashamedly got Deb to pretend she was ill. She turned in an Oscar-winning performance, with me in a strong supporting role as kind friend sacrificing her own pleasure to minister to the sick. The following day she starred in another production. An impromptu performance – gutsy girl making miraculous recovery. Our would-be suitor had informed his mother of Deb's indisposition, and the good lady was amazed and concerned to find Deb back at work so soon.

The things my friends do for me.

We grew up during our A levels, started to take life seriously and stopped playing pranks. No we didn't. It was business as usual. Our pranks just became marginally more sophisticated and we acquired greater skill at avoiding the wrath of teachers. On one memorable occasion at the end of term, the whole of my science option group got hopelessly drunk on the outcome of an experiment that had involved making a fairly punchy form of home-made wine. We had to be given large quantities of water and be marched round and round the school before we were in a fit state to go home. But we didn't get into trouble – the teacher had sampled the wine too!

After A levels we went our separate ways: Deb to Nottingham University to do Sociology, Sue into nurse training and me to Chelsea PE College in Eastbourne. But we didn't lose touch. With Deb in particular, I've remained just as close as I was in those crazy teenage times.

So the next friendly ring on my tree trunk was college, and again some wonderful people who have stuck with me through the intervening years. Going to a PE college is an odd experience. At school you have got used to being the bee's knees sports-wise, and suddenly you're in a place where you are no more than ordinary among lots of jolly hockey stick types competing regionally and even nationally. It's a bit of a shock.

Colleges of Education in those days had a very different culture from universities. Perhaps they've changed since, I don't know. While our university contemporaries were sitting in, freaking out and skipping what few lectures they had whenever it suited them, we were enduring a crowded timetable and a very schooly regime which threatened dire consequences for unauthorised absence. This might have been tolerable if the quality of lectures had been uniformly good, but some of the staff were dreary beyond words. It was George Bernard Shaw who said (unfairly), 'He who can does. He who can't teaches.' College of Education students in the 1970s added the line, 'And he who can't teach, teaches teachers.'

Where we encountered less than sparkling performance

from our lecturers we devised ever more imaginative schemes to avoid their classes. One particularly turgid gym class took place last thing on a Friday afternoon. It wasn't due to finish until 5.30, and most of the class were keen to be on the 5.45 train out of Eastbourne. For all its other delights, Eastbourne out of season was not noted for the vibrancy of its weekend nightlife. There was a rather unkind slogan around at the time: 'Dover for the Continent . . . Eastbourne for the Incontinent.'

So how did we get out of the gym class in time to catch our train? Well, you remember that World War Two escape film where the prisoners use gymnastic equipment as cover for their escape attempt? No, we didn't tunnel our way out from underneath the gym box. We simply moved the box closer to the gym clock, so that when the lecturer wasn't looking one of us could leap up, set it forward half an hour, and convince her that it was time to pack up.

'My goodness, hasn't time flown today.'

There are three special friends from college, Nutch, Mandy and Helen, who have remained very close over the years. Closest of all is Nutch. Her name is really Sarah, but I have this habit of abbreviating the surnames of people I'm particularly fond of, so she'll never be anything but Nutch to me. Having two Helens in the group wasn't a source of confusion as I have never been known to them as anything other than Buckit, and the other Helen swiftly learned to answer to her abbreviated surname, Robs. The four of us met through our various groups at college and got on so well that we decided, with two others, to share a flat in the second year. This so called flat consisted of attic rooms at the top of a large house, six of us sharing two bedrooms.

You wouldn't expect a student flat to have many of life's luxuries. This one had none. On winter mornings there was ice on the inside of the windows, and in the evenings we would have to crouch around a pathetic two-barred electric fire which seemed to consume enough electricity to power half of East Sussex. Even this pitiful source of warmth was cut by 50 per cent when one of its elements gave up the ghost one particularly cold winter's night. This naturally led us to spend more time in the pub, where I developed a deep affection for Guinness.

Our freezing garret was in an odd house with shadowy occupants on the other floors. Rumour had it that one resident kept his wife locked up in the flat and never let her out. Often in the middle of the night you would be wakened by the noise of a spin drier somewhere below. What was it? An illegal drug factory perhaps? They surely couldn't be doing washing at that time of night.

In our flat we had no mechanical washing aids and communal clothes-washing trips had something of the Himalayan expedition about them. When the realisation dawned that there were no clean clothes or bedding in the place, we would pile all the dirty washing into the middle of a large sheet and trundle off down to the laundrette with one of us clutching each corner, the washing swaying around and knocking against our legs like a drunk in a hammock. When this wild procession reached the laundrette, there was no attempt to separate whites and coloureds, denims and delicates. Everything went in together, and everything came out a uniform shade of grey.

Student life wasn't entirely wall to wall fun. There were times when I was low – like the weekend in the first year when my boyfriend from Bath came down, and promptly dumped me in favour of the girl in the room next door – but as far as I can recall they were few and far between. My abiding memory is of us blundering through life shrieking with laughter at every opportunity. At the end of three years Nutch and I escaped to peddle our newly recognised skills on the job market while Mandy and Robs stayed on for the B.Ed year. By the end of 1978 we were all respectable members of the teaching profession.

The 1980s followed a predictable pattern for school and college friends alike – weddings, mortgages, birth announcements and christenings. We matured from bridesmaids into Godmothers and still managed to get together from time to time minus husbands and kids. But even as we bump along into our forties, we have never lost the sense of fun that had thrown us together in the first place. That's very important to me.

There's another ring of friends from my fairly brief teaching career. I'm still in touch with some of the people I worked with at Henry Beaufort School in Winchester, and three summers at a frenetic English language summer school for Eurobrats in Canterbury.

There were some exercises we used with the language students designed around adaptations of Aesop's fables. One of them went something like this:

Aesop was sitting by the side of the road when a traveller came along. The traveller stopped and said, 'I'm on my way to Athens. Tell me what the people are like there.'

Aesop replied, 'Tell me first where you are from and what the people are like there, and I will tell you what sort of people you will find in Athens.'

The traveller replied, 'I come from Thrace, and there none of the people can be trusted. They are cheats and liars all of them.'

'I'm afraid I have to tell you that you will find the people of Athens pretty much the same,' said Aesop.

A short time later another traveller came along the road. He too stopped and said to Aesop, 'Excuse me, my friend. I'm on my way to Athens, and I wonder if you can tell me what the people are like there.'

Again Aesop replied, 'Tell me first where you are from and what the people are like there, and I will tell you what sort of people you will find in Athens.'

The second traveller replied, 'I'm from Thrace and there the people are wonderful – trustworthy, friendly and generous. I love them all.'

'Then I'm happy to tell you, my dear friend,' said Aesop, 'that you'll find the people of Athens much the same.'

I like to think that I've approached new encounters like the second traveller, and I really do believe that if you expect the best of people they will respond accordingly. There is a downside, of course. The hurt is that much greater when people let you down. People like the first traveller are protected from that by their low expectations. There have been occasions in my life when I have felt my trust has been abused. When it has happened I have found it hard to forgive and forget. Nothing particularly unusual about that, I'm sure.

The broadcasting phase of my life is a pretty big ring on the tree trunk, and through it I've developed some great friends. They range from people I met in the early days back in Essex Radio right through to young broadcasters who were still in primary school then. Within the BBC there are those among the household names of whom I'm particularly fond – Des Lynam, Trevor Brooking, Peter Sissons and Rob Bonnet. They've all been great but Trevor has been especially good. Always thoughtful and considerate, he has noticed when I'm down and given support when it's most needed.

I've got to know Des better since I have been ill than I ever did before. He says that I have flowered over the last two years. I don't agree. I think it's just that he didn't know me so well previously. We have the occasional lunch together and he has invited me on to his Radio 2 show. It's always great to be around him, he's such good company.

In December Des and Motty invited me to become an honorary member of a racehorse-owning syndicate. The horse in question is a five-year-old chestnut, Out of the Deep. Apparently when Des first saw him, he said the horse reminded him of Private Pike – gangly and wimpish was the impression. But Out of the Deep has obviously come on a lot since then, for it was a strong and graceful animal that we visited on a trip down to Jim Old's stables in Wiltshire. We all had our photographs taken with him from every conceivable angle. He won't be racing until later in the year and it would be nice to renew my acquaintance with him in a winner's enclosure or two.

Behind the familiar TV faces there is a great team of people who are just as important as those of us who appear in front of the cameras and among them are some of my greatest friends. I've got a special affection for some of the younger people in the team. James Pearce (Jambo) has worked with me on the production side and has been such a tower of strength since illness has made the job harder. But there's a whole group I jokingly refer to as my lads. I'm like a crabby old aunt to them, but I hope I've been able to transmit some of the fun and excitement that I feel about the business and to help them when they are down. I've always cared about grassroots sport and I guess this is a similar thing. It's great to see talented new people coming through.

There's very little sense of established people seeing the younger ones as a threat in my area of work. Things have changed in that respect over recent years. When I started in television there weren't many channels around and so it was very competitive, but in the last five years there has been an explosion of channels and hence more chances. There is a little bit of rivalry between the young ones themselves, and that's where I come in with my auntie routine. I try to help them recognise each other's strengths and build constructive rather than destructive rivalry.

My colleagues have made some lovely gestures towards me recently. The most public was at the *Sports Review of the Year* in December. It had been one of those nightmare evenings. The BBC car which should have picked me up failed to appear, and when I resorted to my own car I was marooned in a ferocious West End traffic jam. With little time to spare I managed to park downstairs at the Queen Elizabeth Centre and to save time I went up the fire escape, only to find myself in an area of cobwebby dereliction. Wow! There I was wandering around, done up to the nines, in a place resembling a scene from *Terminator 2*. I went back down and discovered there was no handle on my side of the car-park exit door, and with my chemo-burned fingers I couldn't manage to prise it open. I really began to panic. Didn't even have my mobile phone with me to summon assistance. Eventually with considerable effort I succeeded in getting my fingers around the door and stumbled through into the sparkle and pizzazz of the awards ceremony. If it hadn't been for Jenny Pitman – more of her later – I would have been a complete wreck.

So there I was, quietly breathing a sigh of relief as the programme got under way, when suddenly the cameras were on me and everyone was clapping. Quite out of the blue, Des had included a tribute to me in the proceedings. I thought I was going to cry and only stopped myself with considerable effort. To the viewer it must have looked as if I was trying to swallow a tennis ball. I felt a mixture of horror, embarrassment and incredible warmth towards my colleagues that they should think of doing this.

In addition to my colleagues, work brings me into contact with all manner of wonderful people from the world of sport. Some of them have become very special to me at a personal level. Jenny Pitman is one who particularly comes to mind. She has been through cancer herself, and her intervention when I made my undignified entrance to the *Sports Review of the Year* provided me with one of those magical moments in my life and started a friendship I really value. As I stumbled past ranks of autograph-hunters at the entrance, my nerves jangling, having just escaped from my subterranean prison, the first person I ran into – literally – was Jenny Pitman and she instantly recognised somebody in need of a mega-cuddle. We walked together into the auditorium with me comfortably enfolded. A life-sized teddy bear could not have done a better job. Since then I have been privileged to visit her at her home in Lambourn, smack next to the stables, and she has demanded a regular bulletin from other colleagues on my progress.

I am just so full of admiration for her on all sorts of fronts. She made it in the tough male world of racing, building up her training business while she was a single mother with two children. As still the only woman to have trained a Grand National winner she is a source of inspiration for the new breed of female trainers. I have heard it said that when she had cancer, she scared it away. Not true. She's larger than life, but a wonderful, warm, down to earth person and not scary at all. Success has not spoiled her in any way and I love the way she approaches life – laughs so readily, cries at what matters and is utterly true to herself.

Jenny retired from training this spring and the business will be carried on by her son Mark. But I can't believe that she will ever disappear from the racing scene. Just to see her talking to her equine charges confirms that this is a person who will always live for horses. She tells me that when she was ill she even asked the vet for advice on her condition and got more answers from him than from a doctor. Now there's an alternative approach I haven't yet tried.

I've flogged the tree trunk metaphor to death now, but the rings keep going on. Parents of Nikki's schoolfriends, neighbours, there's even a ring for my illness itself – fellow-sufferers, people who responded when I particularly needed them, special doctors, nurses and therapists. There are potential friends waiting around every twist in your life, even the unpleasant twists.

So when I was first ill, all these people from the different phases of my life got in touch at the same time. Well that's what it felt like. It was both wonderful and overwhelming. People did it in their own way. Some were emotional, others businesslike and practical. Some were apologetic, not wanting to bother me, or really not knowing what to say to me. Nearly two years on, things have changed a bit. Some people who, in the nicest possible way, were in my face during the early stages have eased off a bit. They understand that I find it difficult and very wearing to sit on the phone for the whole evening. There are those I don't see so often whom I know would be there if I needed them. They realise that I'm not just sitting at home waiting for people to call. Eighteen months ago whole days were taken up with a constant procession of people.

There is no man in my life these days. Plenty of good friends, some that I jokingly call my 'half boyfriends', but no one special companion or partner. In the last two years I have sorely missed having somebody to share the load and help me through in a way that even my lovely daughter, wonderful family and friends can't. Of course, presence of a partner is no guarantee of support through illness. I have heard of plenty who are just unable to hack it, who become bound up in their own needs, and prove to be more of an energy drain than an assistance.

You're probably better off with nobody than with a needy partner. But, hey, wouldn't it be nice to be looked after?

Am I bitter that I should find myself in this position? No, I don't think I am. You can't have everything in life, and that is just something I've missed out on. I am more than fortunate in so many other ways, and there is no point in stewing or harbouring disappointment about relationships that haven't worked out. I remain on good terms with my ex-husband. We had a great laugh together in the early years of our marriage, and he has been very supportive during my illness. For Nikki's sake we tried to avoid the acrimony which so often accompanies a break up, and I think we have largely succeeded. I have some special memories of happy times from my marriage and the other relationships since my divorce. Certainly there have been times, too, when I've felt let down. But hasn't everyone? What pleases me now is that I still enjoy the friendship of the men who have been a part of my life.

Illness changes friendships and family relationships in ways you don't fully appreciate at first. In the emotion and shock of the diagnosis, there is a tremendous coming together and closeness. The attention and concern I experienced in those initial weeks and months was overwhelming and I longed at times for a respite, to be just by myself. People got the message in time and became adjusted to a different sort of relationship with me.

Nobody treats me entirely naturally anymore. Spoken or unspoken, there is always a health assessment attending any conversation. 'Hi! How are you?' becomes much more than a routine introduction. Friends watch the TV screen, paying particular attention to my eyes, looking for any sign that I am better or worse than the previous week. Innocent snippets of conversation become sources of embarrassment. Somebody will say to me, 'We're thinking of going skiing in January' and I'll reply, 'Oh, great. I would just love to do that.' Instantly they're feeling guilty. 'Oh God. Why on earth did I mention that? Not only is she unable to ski anymore, she may not even be here in January.' In all honesty the subject is not really that upsetting to me, but the damage has been done and we both feel the unease. Illness has erected an invisible electric fence around whole areas of normal conversation, feeding unnatural caution into everyday chats.

It's not all in one direction either. A little humour about death and its aftermath helps me to handle it, but I am aware that sharing a joke with others may upset them. Even if I were to comment that I would like 'Always Look on the Bright Side of Life' played at my funeral, it would be a step too far for some. Merely by mentioning my funeral, I would have focused their attention on how they will feel when I have gone. It's called anticipatory grief by those in the trade, I believe. I'm not seriously thinking of having that song, incidentally. It's a bit too irreverent, even for me. But I like to think that if I did, people would say, 'Yeah, isn't that just like Helen,' when they heard it.

All this is hard. Your sense of humour gets lost a bit. Whereas previously I could have a damn good laugh with people, I get conscious now that everybody's being very serious about it all. I don't want all this serious dirge stuff, I'm going through a phase in my life when laughter is just as important to me as it has ever been. I crave a really good, falling about kind of laugh like an addict craves a fix. And yet it would be unrealistic of me to expect others to be right in there able to laugh with me at the same things. I know I'm going to die but I don't dwell on it. They know I'm going to die and they don't dwell on it. They can't laugh about it, whereas I like to think I could now. The other day I was having a chuckle to myself about angels – all the things that an angel can do for you. But it wouldn't make other people laugh. For them it's like any port in a storm. They take it all very seriously.

I'm also very conscious that if I'm not careful I can be indulging in this damn illness all the time. Talking about it, the symptoms I've got today and how I'm dealing with it. It would be so easy for it to become the only topic of conversation. I work hard to make sure that it doesn't happen and, when I'm feeling OK, I can forget about it for a time at work or at a social event. But it can pop into any conversation when you are least expecting it. It's always there lurking about in the background like some particularly obnoxious uninvited guest. I don't go about pretending to be OK when I'm not. If people ask me how things have been, I will tell them the truth: 'It's been absolute shit. I went into hospital and had this treatment or that treatment.' I think it's important, however, not to wallow in it. That does me no good and it does them no good.

Despite a greater awareness of the sensitivities of others, I tend to be more honest with people now than I was previously. I used to care like crazy what others thought about me and I would adjust my opinions too much to what I thought they wanted to hear. Now when I'm asked my view I say what I think. Whether somebody else happens to agree matters much less than being true to myself. I can get quite stroppy when somebody does or says something I don't agree with.

So there you have it. I'm a crabby old bat at times, but fortunately there are enough lovely people around prepared to put up with me. I feel so lucky to have had their support when I needed it most.

9

October 1998 to March 1999

O NE thing about being a cancer patient is that you constantly run into others who are similarly afflicted. Sometimes it can serve to highlight your own fears and concerns for the future, but often it is a very positive and inspiring experience. The visit from Harry Mahon, the Olympic rowing coach, was of the uplifting variety. We had colon and liver cancer in common and so plenty to talk about, he with far fewer tumours than me, but he looked ten years younger than his fifty-six years and was still running and coaching constantly. Harry told me he treated the cancer with respect, practised various alternative therapies, and didn't ever let it get him down.

Before he left, he gave me some shark cartilage which lots of people swear by as a cancer treatment. Apparently, the cartilage contains a substance which inhibits the development of blood vessels. This is necessary in order for the shark to develop a cartilage skeleton which contains no blood supply. The theory as far as cancer is concerned is that without a network of new blood vessels to nourish them, the tumours cannot grow. Shark cartilage comes in various forms – skin patches, enemas and capsules. There is debate about its value in capsule form. Some say the effective agents are broken down in the digestive system. I don't know what to make of it, except to note that the Chinese have been eating the stuff for centuries in the form of shark fin soup, and claim that it works as a rejuvenator and an aphrodisiac. So, even if it doesn't work on your tumours, you can look forward to a good time.

The shark cartilage certainly seemed to work for Harry. This indestructible Kiwi ran the 1999 London Marathon in a pretty respectable time of four hours and ten minutes. He said he was hoping to do it faster, but a virus the previous week knocked him back. It amazes me how anyone can combine marathon training with chemotherapy. He says he manages fifty miles a week, but cuts back to thirty when undergoing treatment.

Another person with cancer whose courage greatly inspired me was Bob Wilson's daughter Anna. She and I had kept in touch over the year since my diagnosis. In November 1998 she was gravely ill, but made it to Bob's *This Is Your Life* which was being filmed at Teddington Studios. She was in a wheelchair and had a lovely smile for everyone. I had the most enormous lump in my throat as she and Bob greeted each other. Anna seemed amazing. I chatted to her and felt so strong physically by comparison. Less than a month later she died. I had spoken to her on the phone a few days beforehand and her courage to face death was evident. It sounds strange, but I still feel her presence. I love Bob and Megs his wife so much, and I still wonder how Bob performs on television despite everything. Anna was the apple of his eye.

Frank Dick, the former British Athletics Director of Coaching, phoned me. He wanted me to climb a mountain near Edinburgh for charity. I had to turn it down, although it was for a good cause. I felt very sorry for myself for being so useless. Frank has a thing about mountains, mental ones as well as physical, and he has been a great help to me in terms of inspiration. I first interviewed him years ago at an event in Yeovil and we have remained in touch ever since. Frank has coached many of the sporting greats: Daley Thompson, Boris Becker, Katarina Witt and Gerhard Berger, to name but four. He is still involved in sports coaching, but has also turned his considerable talents to motivational seminars for business people and the like. When I was first ill he dropped me a line offering whatever help and support he was able to give, and he also sent me a copy of his motivational book, *Winning*.

After I was over the initial crisis, I called and asked him to help coach me through the illness. Coaching may sound like a strange word to use in this context, but what I needed was similar to sports coaching in many ways. The role of a sports coach is to ensure that the athlete is prepared to meet a challenge and come through it a winner. In that process, the mental preparation may be as important as the physical. I want to come out a winner against my rebellious cells, and assistance in preparing myself mentally for that challenge is just as important as it is for the athlete.

Frank reminded me that all achievement is a balance between desire to win and fear of failure. It's so easy to let the fear of failure get the upper hand and to shrink into passivity and negative thinking. You must not only want to win enough, but you must believe that you can win, and be prepared to persist until you do. The most fragile element is belief in your ability to win. You see the effects of its loss every day in the sporting arena. But it's just as important in fighting cancer as it is in winning a tennis match. A belief in my ability to turn a situation around has seen me through many of the crises of this illness.

Another sporting technique which has general applicability is that of visualisation. All good athletes use it. You prepare yourself for a winning performance by visualising yourself achieving it – flowing over the hurdles, clearing the bar at a new height, running smoothly and strongly to a personal best. The tendency I have to set goals and targets is a form of visualisation. In my case a winning performance means simply sticking around for a while longer. Visualising myself being there for Nikki at GCSE time or working at the Sydney Olympics a year later has been an important part of maintaining the motivation to make it. Frank reminded me of the words of JFK – 'If you can't imagine it, you can't do it.'

Maintaining a positive attitude was becoming more and more important as the autumn went on. On the health front there were more bad days than good, and I was relying so heavily on the pain patches and the progesterone. Frequently I would be too whacked to do more than lie on the sofa, unable even to write a letter. Then, a replacement pain patch and I'd be a new person. Very scary. The night sweats were becoming increasingly common, too. Waking up awash, sheets absolutely soaking, sweat even pouring out of my ears; and then being unable to sleep because of the cold after being so wet.

I must begin tomorrow as if it's the start of a new life. Otherwise I'm in danger of going under.

This year has featured the great GCSE build-up in our house. Millions of families will be familiar with the experience: coping with the constant grind, the panic attacks, the sleepless nights. And that's just the parents. The motto in our house has been education, education, education. Where have I heard that before? But it hasn't all been about GCSEs, ineffective nagging on my part and unconvincing assurances from Nikki. In the space of one week, I had four very different educational experiences.

The first was at Nikki's school. The A level choices evening is where teachers turn themselves into sales people to extol the benefits of studying their particular subject. I sat there listening to it all, feeling almost as if I were back at school myself. The Latin teacher was trying to drum up business by waxing lyrical about the success of a former star pupil.

'Marvellous Naomi. I won't say her surname.'

I muttered 'Campbell' to Nikki and we both got a fit of the giggles. There was this teacher solemnly eulogising her ex-pupil who had gone on to get a First in Classics at Oxford and we were convulsed with laughter, tears running down our faces. So wonderfully embarrassing, it quite made my day.

Another day, another school and different emotions. The Endeavour School, a local school for youngsters with learning difficulties, invited me a couple of days later to receive an award as the school's choice of hero. It was a very touching ceremony.

They presented me with a shield and a medal, but I didn't feel in any way deserving of the honour. Listening to the kids singing 'Search For The Hero' was a humbling experience and made me appreciate how lucky I am.

The third experience was a letter from Brighton University, which now encompasses Chelsea College of Physical Education at Eastbourne where I trained as a teacher. They wrote to tell me that they were awarding me an honorary doctorate for my work with women's and disability sport. I was totally thrilled and rang my old college friend Nutch to tell her. She shared my delight but we had a good laugh about the irony of the thing. As a student, my love of sport and having a fun time pushed any academic endeavour to the sidelines. I think they were not distressed to see the back of me in 1977 and, quite honestly, the only way I was ever going to get a doctorate was by being given one.

My final education encounter of the week was an invitation down to Hampshire for the fiftieth birthday party of a former teaching colleague. Geoff Lucas was head of the PE department during my time at Henry Beaufort School in Winchester, and one of the people I've remained in touch with over the years. Pete Green, who had the job before Geoff, was due to make a speech at the party. He had arranged with me that at the end of it he would say, 'And now for the sports news, over to Helen Rollason,' and I would do a spoof sports report based on Geoff's hockey match that afternoon. Unfortunately, it was a bad day health-wise for me, and I didn't feel I could do justice to the gag. I was so tired on the drive down that I had to stop for a sleep in a service station car park. But it was good to see old friends, including Sue Arney, the fourth member of my old PE department, and I started to buck up a bit at the party. Most of the people there were teachers, and I had a really uplifting conversation with a wonderful deputy headmistress.

Deputy heads haven't always been sources of wisdom and comfort for me. I remember a classic encounter on my first day as a newly qualified teacher. I had managed to get the kids lined up ready to go into the classroom. Not an easy job – there was the typical babble of a class on the first day of term with a new and untried teacher. Deputy heads are attracted to noise like moths to light, and sure enough one appeared from nowhere. She silenced the class with a glare, then turned to me.

'And you, get in line.'

There are times in my life when I have longed to be a bit taller.

Throughout the autumn I fretted about my inability to hit top form on air. Just as surfers search for the perfect wave, I came to crave the perfect bulletin. I never seemed to get it entirely right. One day my contact lenses would fuzz up, causing me to labour slightly, another I would stumble over somebody's name: Peter Bromley became Peter Bottomley! One particularly fraught evening, fifteen minutes before the bulletin, the computers went down and we lost all the scripts.

Electrical things keep going wrong when I'm around. Have I been packed so full of toxins that I'm starting to develop an electromagnetic aura?

We had to rewrite everything in fifteen minutes. We managed it, but it was horribly tight. I'm not sure this sort of stress ever did me any good. It certainly doesn't these days.

It had also become more difficult to handle background cock-ups. When you are on air you've got to be able to cope with anything that may go wrong. There are so many things that can happen and you are reliant on others getting it right – the correct piece of film appearing at the right time for example. I found myself stuttering uncharacteristically when anything went a little bit wrong. It's terribly important to me to get my presentation right – a matter of professional pride – and I get very angry when somebody else's cock-up makes me fluff on air. Only one thing makes me angrier and that is when my own failure is the cause.

3rd December, a year since we were burgled. Why do I have this fixation with negative anniversaries these days? Nikki and I went to the House of Lords for a London Marathon promotional event on behalf of Disability Sport England. Nikki had her photo taken with Sporty Spice, and I chatted to Geoff Hurst and Duncan Goodhew. I was very very tired afterwards and went to bed almost as soon as we got back. Slept for ten hours solid and wouldn't have woken then if Nikki hadn't roused me. My toes and fingers were suffering as a result of my new chemo tablet regime and I was feeling the cold very badly.

I had arranged a three-day trip to New York the following week. A chance to do some serious shopping and to meet up with my friend Phil Jones, a former member of the *Grandstand* team who had worked with me on the Paralympics in Atlanta. Out of concern that I shouldn't get too tired, some of the younger lads at work arranged a surprise. They enlisted the support of British Airways and arranged an upgrade to Concorde. It was typical of them, so wonderfully thoughtful.

I was really looking forward to my New York trip, especially with the benefit of Concorde travel. As a child I witnessed the maiden flight of Concorde from Filton near Bristol. I remember standing on tip-toe behind a twenty-foot fence, craning to catch a glimpse of this beautiful machine as it soared into the sky. I never dreamt that one day I'd be privileged to fly in it. And more than thirty years later it is still *the* way to fly. I checked in at the Concorde desk. What luxury! None of those snaking queues of overweight sweating Americans, fractious kids and luggage trolleys bruising your calves. The calm and comfort of the Concorde lounge certainly beats the normal departure lounge, too. There was a complete absence of the prostrate bodies you customarily find stretched across six much-needed seats – people whose midnight flight to Tenerife is now expected to depart at a quarter past seven. None of the muttered arguments between overwrought couples, or the constant clanking of duty free carrier bags either. It really made you think there was glamour in air travel after all. But I couldn't quell the airport anxiety entirely. I was concerned, as ever, about getting to the correct departure gate on time.

'What gate number is it?'

'You're at it already, madam. Departure takes place from this lounge.'

The flight was pretty good, too. No I lie, it was tremendous. I enjoyed every second of it, and I can't remember saying that about a flight for a long time. The high point was an invitation on to the flight deck for the take-off and landing. I felt like an excited ten-year-old as I was ushered forward and shoehorned into a space the size of a small family saloon with a zillion knobs and buttons and a veritable galaxy of indicator lights. Three handsome men were running their hands and eyes over this baffling array and exchanging information partly in English and partly in Martian. Now I thought I worked in a high tech world, but this was a different league. I couldn't believe that the flight deck was virtually unchanged since the plane was first built thirty years ago.

They gave me a seat and a set of headphones and told me that I could stay through the take-off and transition to supersonic flight off the coast of Wales. As all this went on, I could hear through my headphones a babble of instructions which was almost impossible to follow. I reflected on the similarities between this and the talk-back which we receive when presenting on television. I'm sure that, just like us, the pilots become adept at responding to disembodied instructions at the same time as devoting their attention to the job in hand. Unlike us, the penalties for misunderstanding an instruction are a little more life-threatening.

As we passed over Swansea, the captain offered to let me lift the levers that would send the plane supersonic, first one lever then the other. My fingers were raw and painful from the chemo and with all the dexterity of a bunch of bananas I managed to pull both levers at once. Wow! It was as if some giant had given the plane a hefty kick from behind. The pilots thought it was hilarious, but I'm sure that when I returned to the passenger cabin I could smell spilt gin and tonic mingling with fear. I resisted the temptation to shout, 'I didn't do it.'

The upmarket nature of the trip didn't stop with the flight. Phil was at the airport to meet me with a limo and my hotel was no less than the Waldorf Astoria – wonderful reception area, but a very average room. I've heard they do a decent salad though! I shopped till I dropped. Literally. After two days of frenetic shopping, sightseeing and entertainment, my feet were so sore I was unable to walk, and I had to take a wheelchair to the baggage reclaim on my return to Heathrow. Apart from that I felt terrific. I don't think I've ever enjoyed a break so much. I had eaten all the wrong things and totally zonked myself with a round of activity which would have tested the constitution of a healthy teenager, but I felt alive again and that's what matters.

I imagined that New York would see to a lot of my Christmas shopping. I went with two bags, came back with four. But as always there were a thousand and one other things to get. No worries. I like getting ready for Christmas. Once I had recovered my mobility, I quite enjoyed the multiple shopping trips. There was to be no repetition of the previous year's hotel Christmas – home cooking this time. I laboured around Sainsburys piling my trolley with enough food to equip a moderate sized polar expedition. Hard not to when all around you are feverishly doing the same thing. I produced my Christmas card as usual. Every year I draw a little cartoon and get the cards printed locally. This year's not quite as good as last, but I decided it would have to do. My hospital chemotherapy session proved the ideal setting for writing Christmas cards. Marooned in bed, hooked up to the dreaded bag, there are few distractions. I got them all done.

Christmas Eve and almost everything was ready. Mum and Ali arrived and we put the finishing touches to our festive preparation. But I was exhausted and feeling a bit sorry for myself.

'And I need a drink, godammit.'

Why do we put so much emphasis on getting everything right for this one day? There is an unrealistic expectation that we can pile into Christmas a year's worth of family love, harmony and generosity – with a fair measure of gluttony thrown in. And what happens? In homes all over the western world people get on each other's nerves. My house was no exception. Ali and I were uncharacteristically cranky with each other. I became very irritated with her, thinking that she didn't appreciate how ill I was. I stewed about it for quite a while before realising that I was probably being unfair. It's easy to become so bound up in your illness that you fail to recognise adequately that those around you have their needs, too. Their upset can't always be expressed positively. Sometimes hurt comes out in negative ways. My family are brilliant all year round. Mustn't let a bit of Yuletide tension spoil that.

At last, the perfect bulletin. What a way to start 1999. I thought I had lost it professionally, and I can't say how pleased it makes me to know I can still do it.

In mid-January Nikki and I went to Manchester for what might be termed a return match. It was arranged to make up for a disastrous trip the previous April when we had been stuck in a traffic jam for hours, missed half the match, and I stopped believing in God. Yes, honestly! This time we weren't taking any chances. We went up the day before and stayed in the Crowne Plaza. The hotel food was just the sort of stuff I needed to eat. Brilliant natural food, herbal teas etc.

However, I rather blew the benefits by over-indulging to a shameful degree.

We were given the VIP treatment at Old Trafford. Went into the Megastore Museum with nobody in it and chatted with Sir Bobby Charlton during a pre-match delay while technicians struggled to locate the reason for a complete failure of the floodlights. Hey! Electrics going wrong again. Better not own up to my part in this.

I had been invited to draw the raffle at half-time, which meant going out on to the pitch. Big privilege, but scary! Come the interval, we moved from our seats down to the touchline – Nikki breathless to find herself almost within touching distance of her hero, David Beckham. As my name was announced, I scuttled out in front of 55,000 people like a small frightened animal. They gave me a friendly enough reception, which was a big relief I can tell you. Over the years I've heard football crowds shout things that would make Vinnie Jones blush.

A little while after the HEAL charity do in September, Neville Davidson had phoned to ask if I would be prepared to have a cancer care centre named after me. It was an amazing honour, and I was a little unsure at first. It wasn't that I didn't want to help, but it seemed rather presumptuous – the Helen Rollason Cancer Care Centre. I've done a reasonable amount of charity work in the past, lots of media people do, but who am I to have a charity appeal named after me? Dr Davidson took me to see the current facilities at the North Middlesex and fired me up with the improvements a new centre could bring and, yeah, I was sold. No time for false modesty, if my name will raise money to help others, then it's what I'm going to do.

The Centre, for which we are trying to raise £5 million, has objectives ranging from work on prevention and screening to improved diagnosis and treatment. It aims to participate in leading-edge research into new treatments, and to sponsor holistic therapies in conjunction with conventional medicine. Not forgotten either are those people close to the cancer patient. It plans to provide an environment in which family and friends are able to be comfortable and secure.

The launch event was scheduled for 15th January at the Saville Club. I was really struggling in the morning – too weak even to get dressed properly. Put on another pain patch and started to recover slowly. By the time Trevor Brooking called to give me a lift into London I felt much better. What a brilliant line up. Loads of my colleagues, friends, doctors and others who had come to mean a lot to me over the past eighteen months. My speech was pretty impromptu, but maybe the better for that. Ladbrokes came up with a cheque for £10,000 to kick the thing off – a wonderful donation, but frightening to think that it represents just 0.2 per cent of the target. The other 99.8 per cent is going to be a bit of a challenge but I feel in my bones we'll do it.

I seemed to be losing ground in my battle against the bulge. Just couldn't stop eating and was loathing myself, both for the way I looked and for my lack of will power. For all my earnest resolution I would have bouts of eating the wrong things almost defiantly. Boredom was part of the problem. Not working full time meant that I didn't have enough to keep me occupied. The medical regime didn't help much either. I tried to reduce the steroids which were the main culprit, but the discomfort and constant headaches that followed forced me back to them.

The biggest problem of all, I decided, was my addiction to chocolate. I don't use the word addiction lightly. Since December, I've been well and truly hooked. You know that's the case when you have to make forays out to the corner shop for no reason other than to buy a Galaxy, or when you feel compelled to stop and buy some on the way home, even though you've been eating the stuff no more than half an hour before. If I could find the phone number for Chocoholics Anonymous, I'd join up. They would recognise me as a genuine applicant immediately.

I kept making jokes about how fat I'd become – got boobs for the last time in my life. It may have convinced other people that I found it amusing, but it didn't convince me. Underneath I was starting to feel desperate. For donkey's years I'd been a neat seven and a half stone, down to six when I was at my weakest in the autumn of 1997, but now I was up to nine and a half and feeling like a hippo. I was running out of things to wear on air – a bad sign. I tried to seek a solution in exercise, but it left me incapable of fulfilling the normal daily routine.

Four things were getting me down: getting fatter, more tired, breathless and the ever-increasing pain in my liver.

'I've got to make it. I must do something every day now. If I can get through to the summer then things won't be as bad.'

I decided that yoga might be the answer. A bit of a departure for me this – I've always been used to the notion that exercise is no good unless it makes you sweat. But in my delicate state, I thought that something gentle and soothing was in order. Did

I say gentle? Ten minutes into my first class and my muscles were begging for mercy as limbs assumed positions they never knew were possible.

'Odd! Nobody else seems to be finding it a problem. Perhaps I've been put together differently from them.'

I had been invited to be one of the celebrity presenters for the C&A Children of Achievement Awards and was looking forward to it. I have to say, though, that it didn't get off to a particularly auspicious start. I felt sick in the car on the way there and needed lots of deep breaths and water when I arrived. Almost immediately, I was thrown into a cauldron of press and photos – no refreshments, no cosseting, no time to get myself together at all. But the children were utterly amazing. So many cancer patients under fifteen, so many kids looking after single parents alone. Children who had lost parents to cancer, or who were coping with serious disabilities. It did me so much good to see how small my problems were. I can't do justice to almost 150 award-winners in a few words, they were all terrific, but I've got to tell you about a few so you'll understand what I mean. Here are just four.

Ten-year-old Cherrelle Lilley was badly burned in a house fire which killed her father, sister and three younger brothers. Not only has she coped with her own injuries, but has shown the courage and maturity to support her severely traumatised mother through the months that followed the tragedy.

Five-year-old Kyle Barton contracted meningitis and septi-caemia on a family holiday to Tenerife. He developed renal failure, was in a coma for weeks and had to have all four limbs amputated. From being a little boy used to running, playing and being free, he found himself with no arms or legs. And yet he has made an amazing recovery, recapturing normal speech and mental functions, learning to walk on his artificial legs, and to perform many activities with his arm stumps.

Sister and brother Laura and John Hoare are both confined to wheelchairs, having developed an extremely rare progressive disorder that affects walking, speech, sight and hearing. The two youngsters are aware that their situation will not improve and that the prognosis is extremely poor. Despite this they get on with playing a full and active part in life, coping with their pain and seeking no concessions.

I came away from the event feeling truly humble.

My chemotherapy had settled into a routine of two-day spells in hospital every two or three weeks, which was beginning to get me down. I longed to be able to take a break from it for three months and just to rely on the chemo tablets. Apart from the discomfort and inconvenience, I was seriously concerned that my body had become resistant to some of the chemo drugs. Dr Davidson had a different idea. He proposed weekly sessions of just a few hours where I could be in and out during a normal day. Less debilitating and more effective than the two-day arrangement. It also permitted me to follow more easily the advice of Lynne, my chemo nurse. 'Fit the chemo into your life, Helen. Not your life into the chemo.'

Nikki was due to go on a skiing trip. I was pleased and excited for her, I knew she would have a great time, but I was sad about not being able to go with her. I love skiing and the prospect of not being able to do it again is painful. I just hoped, too, that she wasn't going to come back to find me in a worse physical condition. The day of her departure I went to work and didn't do a particularly good job. On the way home I cried – not about her holiday or my failings at work – but about the unfairness of life. I literally sobbed all the way home, something I had never done before. I just couldn't stop crying I was so down.

I stayed in bed for most of the next day, just getting up to watch *Sunday Grandstand*. That cheered me up. The BUPA Indoor Grand Prix was featured and athletics always lifts me. The highlight was Haile Gebrselassie breaking the world record in the 5000 metres. Urged on by a capacity crowd, he only needed to complete the last lap in thirty seconds, but he was impeded by three tail-enders who failed to move out to let him pass. Forced wide on the banked track, he managed to avoid a collision and came in just over a second ahead of the previous world record. The crowd raised the roof. I simply wished I'd been there.

Illness hasn't diminished my love of sport in any way. I enjoy watching it as much as I ever did, and I adore those wonderful inspirational moments – Justin Rose chipping in from God knows how far in the British Open last year, Manchester United scoring those two last-gasp goals in this year's European Cup. These are moments I treasure.

Just to make sure I didn't get too hung up on my own problems, the cat had a tummy upset. Nothing like cleaning up cat crap to make you appreciate the other small joys of life. Perhaps she knew that I had made an appointment to have her spayed. If that was so then it worked for the moment. The vet decided she was too poorly to have the operation that day.

'Sorry, Henna, but you don't get out of it that easily. One cat around the house is quite enough.'

Once again I started to be concerned that I was no longer in control of my life. It's a feeling that surfaces every so often and makes me very angry – the sense that some people treat me like a child because I'm ill. They mean it very kindly and would probably be most hurt if I criticised them for it, but it makes my situation feel worse. Takes my personal pride away. I know that in some areas I'm not as capable as I was, but I don't want to be constantly reminded of the fact. And I'm still perfectly able to manage my own life, thank you very much. Even while I'm feeling irritated by this, I have to wonder whether I've ever been guilty of the same sort of thing. I ponder past relationships and decide I probably haven't. But would I know? It's so unthinkingly easy to do, and I am a bit of a control freak on the quiet. Ah well, there's only one thing I can do. To anybody I've ever treated in this way, I'm really sorry. There!

I can't emphasise too strongly how important it is for people with serious illnesses to maintain some control over their lives. I know I've harped on about it elsewhere in this book, but it's a hobbyhorse of mine. That's one of the things that is so good about the proposed new cancer centre at the North Middlesex Hospital. It aims to give patients that essential element of control and choice. Being associated with something which so closely ties in with my own views gives me a great buzz.

3rd March and I woke up feeling exhausted and worried. No energy and everything was such a struggle. Got pretty depressed about coping with work and life. A massage, two pain patches and some exercises with Keith helped lift the mood. But then I went to see Dr Davidson. Bad news! There were tumours in my lungs now. They were very small, but it was a worrying development. It explained why I had been getting so breathless. I told Dr Davidson how rough I'd been feeling and cried a bit. He gave me a hug and told me not to despair, then came up with a plan to change my treatment again to respond to the developments and, hopefully, to boost my energy as well.

I was a bit wobbly when I went into work the day after the lung news. Felt like crying, and actually did when I told one or two people about the new tumours. But, as ever, I was lifted by those around me. I was working on the World Indoor Championships which were taking place in Japan. Sally Gunnell and Linford Christie were in the studio and we did a great programme. Unfortunately, Britain's athletes in Japan didn't have quite such a good day, with only Colin Jackson delivering his full potential, winning gold in the 60 metres hurdles with a new Championship record. I was pleased with my performance, too. I felt as if I was back in the saddle. The following day I was whacked again, struggled in to work and could barely get around. But surprisingly we had a good bulletin, and that in itself made me feel so much better.

A visit to Mr Ribeiro confirmed that there were four tumours in my lungs – each one less than the diameter of a five pence piece, but two in each lung. They might be operable, but I would need a PET scan and a consultation with another surgeon to check that out. I made the mistake of saying to Nikki, 'We're going to need so much luck now,' and she burst into tears. Stupid of me. But we cried together, and probably that was a good thing.

11th March, my forty-third birthday. Another milestone reached. The day started in Hartswood Hospital where I had gone the evening before for another round of chemo-bashing. I felt OK, despite numerous interruptions during the night with air in the chemo line. Some of the nurses are less proficient than others when it comes to setting up the chemo. Lunch with Hazel was followed by a massage, and then home to open my pressies and finish the day with a lovely supper. I have never had so many wonderful presents and cards on my birthday. In bed by 9.15 and pleased to be there.

The next day I had been invited to a local civic reception. I asked Jambo if he would like to come along with me – he's always brilliant company – but I guess I should have realised that all did not augur well for this event when the cat chewed the acceptance card. I had felt obliged to send it back with a note of apology.

At the appointed hour Jambo duly knocked on my door.

'Blimey, Rollas, you look smart.'

'Blimey, Jambo. What the hell do you think you look like?'

There he stood, ordinary suit, slightly crumpled. He'd clearly come straight from work. Whoops! I realised that I'd forgotten to tell him it was a formal do.

The mayor greeted us warmly at the entrance to the reception, and I mumbled some apology about Jambo's outfit. The mayor said that it wasn't a problem, and then commented that her son would have done exactly the same. Did she think I was

Jambo's mum? Surely not. He thought the idea was hilarious, but my lack of amusement would have made Queen Victoria seem like the laughing policeman.

I laughed later.

Perhaps this is what happens when you get to forty-three.

10

What's the Alternative?

T HERE are literally scores of therapies that have been put forward as alternatives or additions to mainstream cancer treatments. As I've indicated already, I read all sorts of stuff in the early weeks after I learned I had cancer and there was no shortage of advice from others. I wanted to keep an open mind and was more than willing to try things that might help, but I certainly didn't want to become completely cranky. It was also immediately apparent that there was no way that I could go charging off trying anything and everything. Quite apart from the fact that all treatments use up valuable time and energy, you have to select those things which make some sense to you and stick with them, at least for long enough to give them a chance to work.

I'm not somebody who believes that, where cancer is concerned, mainstream treatments can be ditched in favour of alternative medicine. In fact, it's fair to say that my preferred approach is one of complementary therapy rather than alternative. I've read stuff which suggests that the alternatives are at least as effective as the mainstream treatments, but when you're dealing with cancer, I just don't buy it. There's certainly a place for them, but I believe it's very necessary to work with your doctors and to keep them fully informed about what you are doing.

The majority of complementary therapies proposed for cancer patients aim at boosting the body's natural defences, either through dietary control and supplement or by working upon mental well-being. Some, such as Chinese medicine, have been practised for thousands of years, while others are relatively new.

For several years I had been occasionally visiting an acupuncturist called Gillian Kelly. I saw it mainly as a preventative measure and appreciated the increased energy I seemed to enjoy following treatments. A few months before the cancer diagnosis, Gillian told me she thought there was something wrong in my liver and spleen area. She said that I had a yellowish tinge to me, and she thought there was some kind of mass where it shouldn't be in my pelvis. Considering all the tests and consultations I was going through at the time, it's interesting that she should come up with the most accurate assessment of my condition. Naturally this gave me some confidence in her expertise and I have looked to her assistance regularly since the diagnosis.

Acupuncture is one of the main components of Chinese medicine, and has been practised as a conventional treatment there for around three thousand years. The theory behind it is that living energy – known as qi – moves through the body along certain channels or meridians. If this flow is impeded or becomes unbalanced, problems result. The acupuncturist works to correct the flow by stimulating, with needles or other pressure, selected acupuncture points along the meridians. The challenge for western medicine lies with the lack of any scientific proof of the existence of qi or the meridians for that matter. But there is plenty of evidence that acupuncture works with all manner of painful conditions. Not even the greatest acupuncture devotee suggests that it can cure cancer, but it can play a significant part in the relief of pain or nausea associated with chemotherapy.

In recent months I have not seen Gillian so frequently. Conventional treatment has required the insertion of so many needles into my poor body that I have developed an aversion to the things. Even though there is no pain with acupuncture needles, the idea of having them stuck in and wagged around doesn't do a lot for me at the moment. To get around this problem, Gillian has done some pressure point work whereby the acupuncture points are stimulated by finger pressure rather than needles. It helps me relax, eases the pain and aids my digestion. She also uses moxa, a burning herb, which aims to work against the sensitivity and coldness in the hands and feet which you get from chemo.

The second branch of Chinese medicine which Gillian introduced me to was the use of Chinese herbs. As with acupuncture, herbal medicine is not so much about treating specific diseases as promoting the total health of the person through medications which have a general effect. Cancer tumours are seen as the manifestation of general malaise and the action of herbs is towards enhancing the body's natural defences. There is reputable research which has shown benefits for cancer sufferers, including some which appeared to indicate life expectancy improvements for patients with colon and liver cancer. It all seemed perfectly sensible to me and I was prepared to give it a go.

The herbal regimes I follow are, in fact, a Japanese branch of traditional Chinese medicine known as Kanpo. The actual herbs used are the same but there are differences in dosage and the way they are administered. Kanpo also has the benefit of government recognition in Japan which puts a particular emphasis on quality control. From the very early stages following my diagnosis I have taken Eclipta which is a combination of fourteen herbs. This formula is particularly aimed at improving liver function and easing the effects of chemotherapy. I also used fu-zhen therapy which is aimed at boosting the immune system and claims to reduce the tumours.

I still take the herbs, although for half the time I'm not sure that I believe they are doing me any good. There's a strange sensation of feeling slightly trapped by it all. You read the bumf about it and feel, 'Yes of course that makes sense, I've got to try it.' After a time when nothing startling has happened, you begin to wonder. But you're trapped. You tell yourself that you're not feeling appreciably better as a result of the therapy, but you don't know how much worse you might be if you didn't use it. So you carry on popping the pills, and pretty enormous ones they are too, just in case.

Terry Moule, the naturopath I mentioned earlier, came into my life very shortly after I had been diagnosed. He was recommended in a letter I received from somebody who had read about my situation. The letter was one of hundreds extolling the virtues of this or that treatment, but this one stood out. The sort of regime it described made sense to me and there was a sports connection which struck a chord. This man was also an osteopath who had treated many notable sports people such as Seb Coe, Fatima Whitbread and Steven Redgrave. I got in touch with him and he came to see me in hospital.

Naturopathy embraces a pretty wide range of therapies, the overall aim of which is to prevent or cure disease by harnessing the body's own natural healing powers. It seeks to treat the whole person and to work on the underlying causes of disease rather than just the symptoms. In my case Terry set me on a very rigid diet, almost completely vegetarian – virtually no meat or dairy products, lots of fruit and vegetables. The idea of this was to increase the amount of energy available in the body, to boost the immune system as much as possible and to cut down on the presence of toxins in the system. Meat and dairy products contain much higher concentrations of pollutants than vegetables, and also antibiotics and hormones that are a feature of modern farming methods. They are said to increase the number of anaerobic bacteria in the gut which favour the development of cancer cells. The vegetables I went for had to be organic, again for reasons of avoiding the pesticides employed in most vegetable production. The main liquid intake was still bottled mineral water – glass bottles because plastic leaches into the water, so it is claimed.

Just as important as the diet in the early stages was the way that Terry helped me mentally. He encouraged me to live in the moment of now rather than constantly harking back to the past or worrying about the future. He illustrated this wonderfully with an old children's story about a prince and a dragon which I'm going to relate to you. Forgive me if you've heard it before. I hadn't.

Are you sitting comfortably?

Once upon a time there was a young prince who, as princes so often do in stories like this, was wandering around distant lands looking for adventure. He came to a village which nestled at the entrance to a pass between two mountains. On top of one of these was a huge dragon breathing fire and smoke. The villagers were all weeping and wailing and the prince astutely discerned that all was not well with them. He asked what was the matter and they told him that their best fields and crops were through the pass in the next valley and that they couldn't reach them because it meant getting past the dragon. He asked them why nobody had tried to tackle the dragon. They replied that on three occasions they had nominated their best fighter for the task, but that the path up the mountain was so steep that in each case the man had fallen off and died before he reached the top.

The prince was not hugely courageous, but being a helpful prince, he offered to see what he could do. To start with he decided that the most important challenge was to make sure he didn't fall off the path. So he began to make his way up this very narrow path, removing loose stones and obstacles as he went. Every now and then he stopped and took some deep breaths to prevent himself panicking. He noticed that the scenery was quite beautiful up there. He carefully continued picking his way up the path enjoying the scenery as he went. To his surprise he suddenly found himself on the top of the mountain. He looked around and couldn't see the dragon anywhere. Plucking up his courage he called out, 'Come on, dragon, where are you?' and he heard a little squeak from close to the ground. Looking down, he saw that by his left foot was a tiny little animal which he picked up and found that it was a baby dragon.

'Where's your big brother, little dragon?' said the prince. 'I've come up here to fight him.'

'There's only me here,' said the dragon.

'But you can't be the dragon that's frightening the whole village.'

'Oh yes, that's me.'

'Well how on earth can you do that?'

'I'm able to do it because of my name,' said the dragon.

'What is your name?'

And the dragon said, 'What Might Happen.'

From a distance, What Might Happen is terrifying and we get so frightened of it that we fall off the path before we ever meet it. But if you live in the present and do what you can to the best of your ability, when you meet your dragons you will nearly always find that they are ones that you can pick up and deal with.

Terry also taught me a lot about rationing and conserving energy to fight the disease, something I hadn't thought much about in my previous flat-out lifestyle. He made me realise that there is an unconscious element to energy expenditure which can have a pretty serious effect upon our well-being. As Terry described it, we each have one amount of energy which you can liken to a bank account. In the course of our daily lives we pay out energy cheques from morning to night – working, enjoying ourselves, running the home – that's the energy expenditure we are aware of. The other element of our expenditure is more like direct debits – regular unconscious payments to maintain essential services: digestion, assimilation, elimination, healing and repair. If we carry on paying out big cheques when we're low on energy, then the direct debits don't get paid properly and we don't digest, assimilate, eliminate, heal and repair as well as we should. The result may be a breakdown in the immune system.

So the answer is to manage your energy. Pay out small cheques and make sure there is always enough to meet the direct debits. Overdrafts aren't allowed on energy accounts.

This whole regime helped me to feel more in control of my body and what was happening to it. That's a very important feature of alternative therapies generally. As a cancer patient, all manner of things are done to you – very technical things which turn you into an object to be injected, probed or zapped by machines. Embarking on dietary or herbal treatments enables you to say to yourself, 'OK, this is my body, and I'm taking some control over its treatment.'

For several months after my initial diagnosis I rigidly adhered to the regime, and I certainly believe it did me a great deal of good. The natural, non-toxic treatment was in sharp contrast to the poisonous concoctions that made up the chemotherapy. Being in a position to manage the diet myself gave me a very positive handle on the disease. A major weapon in defeating it. But in time that changed. I started to feel that it was doing me damage psychologically. It was almost as if I would die if I didn't adhere to it in every last detail. Even eating a chocolate biscuit would fill me with the most enormous guilt. I was unsure how much good the regime was doing me, but petrified about the consequences of abandoning it. And I craved the forbidden foods with the obsessiveness of a child whose parents have banned sweets. The sequence of events went like this: crave chocolate, give in to temptation, feel bad, curse my weakness, become rebellious, won't let this dictate to me, eat more chocolate.

Lately I've become a bit better adjusted. I give myself treats but don't feel quite so guilty about them. My job is a very sociable one with frequent opportunities for nice lunches, and I really can't be doing with constantly scouring the menus for something which will fit my diet. I still follow the main strands of the diet but without the previous rigidity. I eat lots of fresh fruit and vegetables and my main protein intake comes in the form of fish. I consume very few dairy products and hardly any meat, just occasionally a piece of chicken.

The link between food and survival is a very direct one in my case. I only have a tiny piece of liver still working. If it continues to function well I'll stay alive, but if it packs up, I'm a goner. The more work I give it to do, the sooner it's likely to pack up. The suggestion is that some oily foods, meat and dairy products included, make the liver work harder. Needless to say alcohol is completely out – not much good for the liver at the best of times. It's worth noting that an intolerance to alcohol was the first hint I had that something was awry, two or three years before my cancer was diagnosed.

So there is a deal of logic to it and, of course, diet is now acknowledged to be a huge factor in the potential development of cancer, but how important it is when you already have cancer at an advanced stage is a matter of dispute. Some doctors have suggested that it might help, others have more or less told me to eat what I like. When you haven't got much life left, you might as well have a good time.

In the autumn of last year I was introduced to Eric Llewellyn and Peter Wallace who run a company called Nature's Own which has had a close relationship with the Bristol Cancer Care Centre. Eric has helped me to adjust my approach to diet, so that I feel more in control and less psychologically affected by my weakness for treats. His approach allowed for some compromise on what I ate, recognising that the stress and internal conflict that can result from rigidly trying to maintain a 100 per cent healthy diet may cause more damage than my tendency to stray from the foods that are good for me. It was better in his view for me to be building myself up through a predominantly healthy diet, and doing the occasional bit of damage, than suffering the negative energy that resulted from the attitude I was beginning to develop towards food. Eric's approach was to recommend the foods that were going to suit my body type and the nature of my illness, and then to ask me which aspects of these recommendations I didn't like. He would then work on these to try to find alternatives. The notion that I could enjoy myself eating was hugely welcome and helped me get myself back on track.

Nature's Own also introduced me to a vitamin and mineral regime in a natural food-based form which the body is able to handle and which, they claim, offers benefits not available from synthetic vitamins. It's the regime I'm still following.

People constantly write asking what diet I'm on. I find myself a little reluctant to make recommendations from my own experience. It's not that I don't want to help people. If I thought I had the answer I'd be happy to walk around Oxford Street with it emblazoned on a sandwich board. I just don't want people to get the idea that there is some form of dietary Holy Grail, and I don't want them to get trapped into that way of thinking where the diet starts to control your life. I believe that a variety of the things I've done may have worked to prolong my life, but I'm not convinced that any single one of them holds the key, and I'm very conscious that we are all different. What works for me may not for somebody else, and vice versa.

I wouldn't want anyone to take that as a signal to do nothing. I passionately believe that there are all sorts of things you can do, and managing your diet is most certainly one of them. But make it *your* diet, make it *your* positive campaign, remain in control of it *yourself*. Don't expect to seize a magic off-the-shelf package from me or anybody else.

I have heard of doctors being offended or dismissive when patients try other things. Mine weren't at all. Quite the contrary, in fact, and I was very impressed with that. Dr Davidson was particularly encouraging. The HEAL cancer charity of which he is the Chairman takes a holistic stance, and he believes there is a lot to be said for alternative medicines. One thing I'm clear about is the need to be open with doctors about any alternative therapies you may be considering. Some seemingly innocuous treatments can make matters worse. Aromatherapy oils penetrate the skin and may clash with other medication.

171

Massage can stimulate the release of cancer cells to other parts of the body.

In the spring and summer of 1998 I was drawn into several experiences of spiritual healing. In each case the suggestion came from somebody I knew and was accompanied by a certain amount of scepticism on my part. But I was pretty desperate to prolong my life, and was prepared to have a bash at things I previously would not have considered. They were very varied experiences, some moving, sublimely comforting and practical; others distinctly uncomfortable or quite weird. Let me tell you about three different encounters.

The first was a healing service at a rather cultish church. Nikki and I had been invited by somebody who had recently got into religion in a big way. The whole thing was pretty powerful stuff and I quickly began to wonder what I had let myself in for. The singing and praying were far more intense than any service I had previously been to, and the sermon just seemed to go on and on. I reckon that it lasted about an hour, but it was one of those occasions where you start to lose track of time. Then the minister started to heal people – a guy who couldn't raise his arms, a chap in a wheelchair, a blind man. Everything was extremely theatrical and emotionally charged, people brought out of the congregation and 'healed' in front of us, even video cameras rolling while it took place. The sight of one poor bloke being hauled out of his wheelchair made you want to cry, and they added to the drama by bringing on his wife and kids. Then the blind man was spectacularly healed. We were all able to read about him before he came up, and when he sat down he could read about himself, too.

After these people who had been in some way pre-selected, there was a call for anybody else who wanted to come up. Nikki said, 'Go on, Mum,' and pushed me forward. We were both crying at this point and I didn't want my naked emotions displayed in public, but I went up. The minister held me and said I would be healed, and I have to admit that my awareness of the congregation dissolved. Then I was carted off by the minister's wife who also held me and wanted to know my details. It may be unfair of me towards people who really believe in what they are doing, but I actually got the feeling that in some way I was being set up as a high-profile convert. Both Nikki and I found the experience very uncomfortable, and returned home like washed out dish rags.

A totally contrasting encounter came via a good friend of mine who runs a pub locally. Out of the blue one day an acquaintance said to her, 'You've got a friend who needs my help.' Sue, the landlady, thought of me, and so I was introduced to Laura. She didn't know me from Adam, didn't watch sport or anything like that, wasn't interested in the fact that I was well known, as I'm afraid some people are. She just wanted to help, although she was concerned that the rapport might not be right, and the initial visit was just a one-off.

She came to my house. It was apparent that we viewed life from different perspectives, but there was an unmistakable chemistry there, and something about her that I immediately warmed to. I have continued to see her every few weeks since, and regard her as very special. I still know nothing about her other than her first name. I don't know what she does, but she makes me feel better. She uses her hands and it seems as if there is enormous heat coming from them. And she talks to me, not about the disease so much, but about the spiritual power which she believes still has a mission for me. She believes that the angels have work for me to do and that I won't be popping off just yet.

Whilst I don't quite share Laura's beliefs in God and angels, I do believe in some sort of power, and the things she tells me are both comforting and positive. They are what I want to hear. She wants nothing in return except for me to get better, absolutely refuses to take any money. In a world where everybody seems out to make a buck, it's a wonderfully refreshing thing to meet somebody with her kind of attitude. Meeting her is a privilege I would not have enjoyed had it not been for my cancer, and I'm really grateful for the opportunity.

You might wonder, if I don't entirely believe in the religious spiritual side, how I can think that healing is doing me good. Well I don't entirely know, but in circumstances like those I've described above, it certainly appears to work. Medical experts point to some real physical consequences of prayer and healing which are quite earthly and logical. To start with they say that, in just the same way as meditation or massage, it brings about what they call the relaxation response and reduces stress. Everybody accepts that high levels of stress can make you ill – I think it contributed in my case – and there is strong evidence that in situations of low stress the body's immune system can be strengthened. Prayer and healing also introduce a sense of order about life. You are not on your own in this struggle. There is some care and protection beyond that which your friends or doctors can provide. This is likely to foster a more positive attitude towards the future, and there is lots of evidence that attitude has a great deal to do with recovery. So for anybody who has wondered about it, but doesn't entirely buy the religious bit, I would say approach it with an open mind, and if the healer and the circumstances are right, you may be surprised.

My encounter with psychic surgery was a different experience again.

Keith Morton, my exercise trainer, told me about a psychic surgeon who was based in Chelmsford. This man, Stephen Turoff, was world famous for his amazing results and people came from all over to see him, coachloads of people. There he was just ten miles down the road from me. Keith counted himself as something of a sceptic, but suggested it was an opportunity I shouldn't pass up. Much against my better judgement, I agreed.

'OK, but you've got to come with me. This sounds a bit wacky.'

I had read a bit about psychic surgeons — people who operate without any instruments, anaesthetic or pain. Their hands appear to delve into the patient's body and in some cases they will appear to pull out offending items, cancerous tumours for example. They have frequently been condemned as frauds, and the apparent removal of foreign matter has been put down to nothing more than conjurer's sleight of hand, a concealed piece of animal meat slipped into the palm at the appropriate moment. And yet for all this, there was apparently significant evidence of success and that made it worth looking at. I knew they were very popular in South America and the Philippines, but I hadn't expected to encounter one in Chelmsford.

Well the bit about people from all over the world was true. The place was absolutely packed with people of all nationalities. Stephen Turoff was not quite what I had expected. Nothing exotic about him. With his strong cockney accent, long hair, goatee beard and somewhat bloodhound features he rather more resembled an ageing rock musician than a renowned guru. I was pleased to discover that with this particular psychic surgeon there would be no pieces of flesh plucked from my innards. He works with a healing ash, and maintains that the spirit of a German doctor is using him to do the surgery. If this is so, then the late lamented physician must have worked himself into an early grave, because the process takes no time at all. It's all over in two or three minutes. What wouldn't the National Health Service give for a few live doctors who could work at this speed.

Stephen was a friendly enough character, and kept up a lively patter while treating me, laughing and chatting, but at £20 for three minutes work he could afford to smile. Certainly there was the strange illusion that his hands were going into your body, but I have to say that I came away even more sceptical than I had been beforehand.

For me this is a treatment that does require a level of belief above and beyond. If you are able to believe in it, then I'm prepared to concede that it may actually do you some good. It's like the placebo effect. People given totally ineffective sugar pills have responded because they believed they were being given drugs to fight their condition, and I guess that if you can believe in psychic surgery, then the reduction of fear and stress may actually help to boost the body's natural defence systems. But I couldn't believe in it.

If I were to sum up my whole approach to alternative therapies it would be this. Provided I can see some element of sense in it I'm prepared to have a go. There may be things that I wouldn't have previously considered, even run a mile from, but one of the few positive things about this disease is that it has expanded my horizons. I'm conscious that people in my position are vulnerable and can fall victim to quackery, and for that reason I try to maintain a questioning stance. But you can't rely all the time on science and logic. Sometimes you have to take a bit of a leap in the dark.

My approach has changed a little recently. When I was first told I had not much time to live, I was prepared to try anything. For some reason I don't now quite feel the desperation that I did. So I'm not going mad to look for new ways of dealing with this illness. I'm not reading everything and saying, oh God, I must have this or that. I've selected from those things which make sense to me and it would take something pretty stunning to get me into any new treatment now. You simply can't fit it in and lead a normal life.

I still get letters from people telling me about this or that amazing therapy, but there is no way of proving their claims, because at the same time as they are having whatever the therapy might be, they are also receiving conventional treatment and possibly doing other things, too. The only way to arrive at firm proof would be to have groups of people who only received one form of treatment. That's clearly out of the question when people's lives are on the line. Somebody once said that 50 per cent of advertising is wasted, but he couldn't work out which 50 per cent. You could say the same about alternative therapies, or all cancer treatment for that matter.

11

March to May 1999

THE satisfaction at reaching my forty-third birthday didn't last long. A few days later I was feeling terribly depressed about my condition, more negative than at any time. I had no energy, felt so physically ill and mentally weak. I was raw and on the verge of tears constantly. I wondered whether this time I would be able to turn it around. I told myself that I could be justifiably proud of myself if I was able to. It was a matter of shifting my perspective, seeing this as a phase and not the end. Others did their bit to help me break out of it. Neville Davidson phoned and urged me to remain mentally strong. Eric Llewellyn came over and encouraged me back on track. I realised that part of my negativity lay in grief for the person I used to be – slim, busy, energetic. It wasn't helping me trying to hang on to that person. I needed to let her go now.

I had a great time at the Television and Radio Industries Awards. There were 1200 people there and I chatted to all sorts from Trevor McDonald to Bob Wilson. Physically I was still shot to bits but mentally feeling stronger. I put my new resolution about letting go of the old Helen to the test by cancelling a game of golf that had been scheduled for the following day. It was a big relief, I was just not up to it. But it felt very sad, like I was saying goodbye to an old friend.

It's cerebral activity for me in future.

Who do you think you're fooling, Rollason?

Well a trip to Dubai could be cerebral I suppose, but it was really all about pampering my body. I went with Ali for a week away from the phone and the dreary British April. It's amazing what a difference a change in climate can have on me. Solid sunshine and a temperature above 30 degrees soon had me thinking about a bit of gentle exercise. I couldn't resist venturing on to the immaculate golf course with peacocks wandering around the fairways. The first attempt was pretty execrable, but I got better and by my third outing I was beginning to regain my confidence. Was it just two weeks ago I'd thought of hanging up my clubs? It wasn't all plain sailing. A very rebellious tummy kept me marooned around the hotel for the first three days, eating ultra-safe food. I pinpointed the culprit – chemo tablets – and gave them the heave ho. Quickly felt much better, and started to sample some of the local colour. Well, as much of it as you can get in a place which is geared to providing neat parcels of tourist-friendly culture at sky-high prices.

I rode a camel, or rather, lurched around on the back of one for ten minutes, had my leg painted with a henna tattoo and went to an 'authentic' Arab beach party. I drew the line at the belly dancing – brilliant exercise, but my belly is not currently for public display. I had never visited Dubai before and was fascinated by the place. It's competing strongly in the tourist market with excellent facilities catering to international tastes. But for all that this has driven a whirlwind through its historic culture, there are strong elements of the traditional male-dominated society still very much intact.

Hmm! Sounds rather like the BBC Sports Department.

I came home to find that my tumour activity levels had escalated to a worrying degree. Not since my abortive liver operation had things been so busy in me. I had hoped to be able to leave off all treatment for a while, but unfortunately that was out of the question. Hey, ho! Hospital again with some tough chemo to try and stabilise things.

I was saddened to hear that my dear old friend Edie had died. Yet another special person in my life gone. I stayed in Edie and Claude's house when, in my second year at college, I spent a term on an exchange with Dalhousie University in Halifax, Nova Scotia. Canada in winter was a totally new and exciting experience for me, and I adored the warmth and humour of my lovely hosts. Our friendship lasted through the intervening years, and Edie seemed like such a permanent feature. It was hard to think of her not being around any more. Over the next few days I spent a lot of time recapturing her face and her laugh in my mind.

When Ali and I were in Dubai, we spent some time taking stock of our lives and drawing up resolutions for when we got back. One of mine was to do something about the Saturday night sports roundup. I had reluctantly come to the conclusion that it was not doing my health any good at all. The presentation bit is only five minutes, but it's the ten-hour stint beforehand that knocks you out. By the time we got to the bulletin at 10.25 p.m. I was knackered. Strangely, after the bulletin I would feel as high as a kite – something to do with the belt of adrenaline it gave me I guess – and I would go home buzzing with energy. The penalty would come the next day. Late nights come back to haunt me with a vengeance.

For all that, I was reluctant to bow out from it. On the busiest sporting day of the week, the Saturday sports news has always felt special. It's fun to be the one to bring the latest on big events. Peter Sissons and Michael Buerk are just great to work with, and the newsroom is different at weekends, too. It's much quieter and there is a greater sense of camaraderie than at other times of the week. So imagine my surprise and delight when, shortly after we returned from holiday with resolutions fresh in our minds, up popped a new proposal.

'I don't suppose you'd be interested in doing a sports review for the new Friday evening *Six o'Clock News*, would you?'

'Would I!'

Just what I needed to make the right decision about Saturdays. I had worked with Huw Edwards before on Breakfast and was very relaxed with him. He with me, too, I think. We shared an abiding hatred of the 4 a.m. starts. Perhaps early evening suits both our body clocks.

The BBC is very loyal to its staff, and I have been fortunate in being on the receiving end of that loyalty over the last couple of years. Many organisations would have written me off or at least sidelined me, but the Beeb has been prepared to take a risk on my health. I'm grateful for it. What's more, there are so many people in the organisation who really care – not just among the foot soldiers – there are some fun guys at the top.

A few suits in the middle, I'm afraid, but that's probably the same in any organisation.

I wouldn't want you to run away with the idea that absolutely everything about the BBC is wonderful. The downside to its loyalty is a certain amount of complacency, a belief that it can carry on doing what it has always done regardless of competition. Some of the recent problems of BBC Sport are down to that in my view. I was very sad for the people involved when we lost the motor racing, but then it happened again with the cricket and that was even more of a shock. It seemed as if the lessons from the first time hadn't been heeded.

Sunday 18th April was London Marathon day and I had been given the honour of starting the wheelchair race which kicks off fifteen minutes before the mass start. David Hemery, the 1968 Olympic 400 metre gold medallist and now the President of Athletics UK, was the starter for that. Blackheath on marathon day is a sight to behold. Athletes converge from all directions carrying their regulation plastic kit bags until the whole of Blackheath and Greenwich Park is a seething mass of humanity. The stink of embrocation rises in the cool morning air and everywhere there are people stretching, people jiggling in long snaking queues for the portable toilets, and those who can't wait peeing behind every available bush.

London vies with New York for the largest marathon field in the world, and this year there were around 32,000 starters from the 40,000 accepted for the event the previous autumn. The drop out is typical for an event of this size – those who are ill or injured, plus those whose optimism at entry time was greater than their dedication since. I had been there before, helping to cover the event for the BBC. Pre-race chats with celebrity runners and pantomime horses were followed by mid-race interviews on the run, thrusting a microphone at the oldest, the youngest and the craziest, while matching their pace along the route. No chance of doing that now; this time I was part of the show.

Being a starter for an event like this isn't just a matter of turning up and pressing a button at the right moment. There's a great pre-race build-up, and the organisers looked after me wonderfully, starting with a lovely meal the evening before. Lots of top athletes were there. Not those who were actually running the marathon, they were already tucked up in bed, but people like Jonathan Edwards, Fatima Whitbread, Steve Backley and Iwan Thomas. Some of them were acting as starters for the mini marathon, the 2½ mile races for schoolchildren along the final stages of the marathon course.

The morning dawned very chilly but dry with just a gentle breeze – perfect conditions for doing a marathon. It was a 6.30 start for me in order to be at the wheelchair tent by 8 a.m. It's fascinating to watch athletes going through their pre-race preparations. Every little detail has to be right, and for wheelchair marathon competitors this is a matter of tuning not only the body, but the chair as well. I watched as they pumped up tyres, filled water bottles, and fitted bits of the three-wheeled bikes together to suit their needs. I had it easy. All I had to do was to wait until 9.15 and, on a signal from Dave Bedford the organiser, to press a pretend starter button. The klaxon which should have blasted them into action emitted a feeble and embarrassing squawk. By the time it found its full voice the athletes were already disappearing in the direction of Woolwich.

While they set about the challenging 26.2 mile course, I was able to watch the mass start at 9.30, and then, with scarcely the need to walk for more than a few yards, was transported to the Mall in time to watch the finish of both the wheelchair and foot races. First home in the wheelchair race was Heinz Frei of Switzerland, who sprinted down the Mall just ahead of Frenchman Jeannot Joel. Britain's David Holding who had been hoping for a fifth win in the event, had to be content with third place. Swedish superstar Monica Wetterstrom, who won two years ago, was victorious in the women's wheelchair event, with Britain's four-times winner Tanni Grey in second place. Tanni was due to get married a couple of weeks afterwards, and if that's not a reason for a slight distraction from her training, I don't know what is.

The finish to both women's and men's foot races was exciting and inspiring. Joyce Chepchumba from Kenya powered home in a new world best time for a women-only race and reasserted her authority on the event she won so closely in 1997. In one of the strongest men's marathon fields ever assembled, Morocco's Abdelkader El Mouaziz knew that his lack of a sprint finish meant that he would have to take on the pace at an early stage. He ran bravely from the front and ploughed a lonely furrow over the last ten miles He was able to hold off a late challenge from 1997 winner Antonio Pinto and won the men's race in a personal best of 2:07:57. Unfortunately, he missed the course record by just two seconds, and undoubtedly blew it by

185

indulging in some premature celebration waving over the last couple of hundred yards.

After the élite athletes came the club runners and then the masses of slower runners pouring down the Mall. People of all ages from eighteen to eighty-six. There were more than a thousand old age pensioners in this year's race. Isn't that amazing? I'm full of admiration for anyone who can contemplate tackling a twenty-six mile marathon course, and the sight of so many thousands pouring across the finish line is truly uplifting.

I have to take my hat off to the organisers as well. The whole thing goes like clockwork. Not just for celebrity starters either. The finish marshals have to cope with several hundred finishers a minute during the peak time. Each one receives a correct finishing time, photograph of the moment they cross the line, medal, congratulations, drink and goody bag. And within a couple of hundred yards of the finish is a truck carrying their kit bag which they last saw at the start. That's a feat of some military precision. I had a brilliant day, and finished it off by presenting the trophies for the wheelchair race with Sports Minister, Tony Banks.

The next week there was a trip to Rome to film a programme about women football commentators for the BBC2 Saturday night *Correspondent* spot. First stop was the Olympic Stadium for a European Cup Winners' Cup match between Lazio and Locomotive Moscow at which I was due to meet Sister Paulo. I'm not joking, this was a real live football-commentating nun. In the semi-darkness of the stadium, and to the background cacophony of thousands of excited fans, I conducted an interview which could have been straight out of

Monty Python. Sister Paulo talked to me, Lazio scarf wrapped around her habit, huge pot of popcorn at her elbow, and a procession of fans coming up to kiss her hand. Frequently during our conversation she would break off in mid-sentence to emit a whoop of joy or agonised groan. These startling outbursts were, of course, linked to the on-field action rather than to anything I was asking her, and the translator didn't need to put them into English. When it was all complete, we had to do it again. The cameraman decided that there hadn't been enough light. Annoying, but that's television.

In Italy, where the two predominant institutions are football and the church, this lady almost seemed to be uniting two religions. Apparently, she once played football and then coached it before moving into television punditry. She says it is her way of keeping in touch with the young poor people of Rome. I liked her. She was as nutty as fruit cake, but obviously much loved by the Italian fans.

Women commentators are much more common in Italy than is the case in Britain, or other countries for that matter. But I'm afraid it hasn't a lot to do with equality of opportunity. It's all about ratings and Sister Paulo is far from typical. The prevailing trend is to feature glamorous and alluring female commentators whose knowledge of football statistics comes a poor second to their ability to display the vital kind. The television companies say that the predominantly male viewers enjoy looking at them. Hey, who would have thought it? For all this triumph of appearance over expertise, it's almost unknown in Italy to have women doing the sort of general sports presentation work that I do.

But not all the female Italian commentators are bimbos. I met one highly respected female sports journalist, Donatella Scarnati, who used to work week in week out on match commentary. Back in the late eighties, she was reckoned to be the first female football commentator in the world, and had a reputation for an encyclopaedic grasp of football facts and figures. Despite that, Donatella reckons that female commentators have the edge over men in their ability to focus much more on human angles rather than statistical information bashing. I observed her commentating on a match, and her style was very alien to British commentary expectations. Motty it wasn't!

There is much more skill to commentating than is often appreciated. It's not necessary to have been a good player, but you do need a particular kind of communication ability, plus a lot of hard work in order to develop the facility for spontaneous identification. I don't know how they do it. I can barely spot my own cat at the bottom of the garden.

I was interested to talk to senior figures in British television sport to get their views on the prospect of female commentators over here. Bob Shennan, the Head of BBC Sport, told me that he believes there is room for women to develop a different commentary style rather than trying to emulate the traditional male approach. There's no reason why women cannot do the job at least as well as men. A psychologist I interviewed on the programme pointed out that women are more verbally fluent than men, and there's no doubt that there are plenty of women about who know their stuff when it comes to football. I think the main stumbling blocks are fear of failure and the reaction of men. Ten years ago there were no female football journalists, and that has changed. Let's hope before too long we start to see female commentators.

And what of Rome? Brilliant, but most of what I saw was at breakneck pace. Our driver Francesco fulfilled every stereotype of Italian drivers. Dark, dishy and talking non-stop, he careered through cobbled streets, foot to the floor, seemingly oblivious of the hundreds of scooters, restaurant tables and strolling pedestrians that in any normal town would have reduced traffic to a crawl. When we put together a sequence in a red Mini Cooper for our last piece of filming on what we had dubbed 'The Italian Job', it seemed pretty tame by comparison.

As ever there was a price to pay for all the feverish activity and unhealthy food. Pasta, pastry, peanuts and hardly a scrap of fish or fruit. I was disgusted with myself. What's more I came home to the news of Jill Dando's death which shocked me terribly. The day after my return I felt awful. Night sweats, weak and useless.

'So, if assignments like this make you feel so bad why do you do them?' I hear someone ask.

Because the ups make the downs bearable. They really do. Doing something with your life is what it's all about, and anything else would be a recipe for swift decline. Besides, there's another up just around the corner.

Yep! The Royal Television Society Awards. Brilliant! Met loads of friends and had a quite superb evening. And then two days later I went to the Charlton Athletic ground to watch the women's FA Cup. I presented the Cup and met all the players.

'A pretty OK afternoon all in all, and thank God I'm beginning to feel better again. My tumour levels are still around 3000 but at least they're not going up.'

Over the years I've interviewed hundreds of top sporting stars. There haven't been so many of late, what with not working full time, and lacking energy to zip around the country as much as I used to. But I do find that interviews these days will often give me insights into my own life and the way I am dealing with my illness. I talked to Britain's top 400 metre runner Iwan Thomas in early May. He was telling me about his diet and training regime and particularly about the way in which hypnotherapy helped him to get his mind focused last year after a poor start to the season. He went on to have the best season of his career, becoming the European and Commonwealth Games Champion, as well as winning his event in the World Cup in South Africa.

If the right focus and attitude can have a world-beating effect on athletic performance, then there is every reason for believing that similar benefits may exist in the fight against disease. Nobody seriously suggests that you can think away cancer cells, but I really believe that my attitude can have a lot to do with how rapidly the disease is able to progress, and hence how long I may live. Hypnotherapy is also widely considered as an effective means of easing the effects of cancer treatments and improving quality of life. I haven't yet tried it, although I did make contact with a practitioner recently. Unfortunately she had a rather negative effect on my mental attitude, and my pocket, too. She charged me forty quid for what was no more than a sales pitch. I'm sure I was just unlucky. I'll look elsewhere and give it a bash. If it can make me run the 400 metres like Iwan Thomas, I'm all for it.

Another interview I did a few weeks earlier was with Alex Ferguson, the Manchester United manager. As I write this, his knighthood has just been announced, and richly deserved it is, too. Here is another great advertisement for the power of attitude. In his case it's the ability to transmit self-belief to others and to turn that into consistent team success in one of the most cut-throat businesses around.

The interview was timed for mid-morning, which meant a crack of dawn start and a bleary eyed attempt to prepare my questions in the back of a BBC car zipping up the M6. A quick stop to adjust the make-up – wouldn't want to frighten the man – and it was in through the hallowed portals of Old Trafford. It's a remarkably friendly place, which comes as a surprise in Premiership football, but to tell the truth I was pretty anxious about the interview. I didn't feel one hundred per cent sharp and I knew how rare it was to get a long interview with Alex these days. He is reputed to have no great affection for the BBC and I was quite surprised, and delighted, that he was prepared to do an interview with me.

We arranged to hold the interview in the boardroom and tried to make it look as cosy as possible by rearranging the sofas. Whose comfort were we seeking, Alex's or mine? My anxiety wasn't eased by his lateness. He breezed in forty minutes after we were due to begin. His body language was initially intimidating, and he wanted to know what the interview was about. 'Well, it's about you actually, Alex,' I gulped. But for all the gruff exterior he's a sweetie underneath. I later learnt that he'd cut himself shaving that morning, so my appearance probably felt like just one more irritant in a bad morning. After a couple of questions he relaxed and couldn't have been more interesting to talk to. He has an energy for life that I can only envy at the moment.

We talked about his great relaxation, horse racing. It would appear that the race track is a place where he can lose himself. His eyes sparkled as he related stories of horses bought and sold. He even gave me a racing tip for a horse that was running the next day – a dead cert.

I put a large bet on it to win.

It came in second.

Never mind. It just goes to show that even Alex Ferguson can't get everything right.

12th May and I was feeling pretty rough, having been awake all night. My mood wasn't helped by finding the wing and guts of a bird on the kitchen floor. Yuk! Henna's new-found opportunity to roam in the early morning clearly isn't a good idea. I did a bit of work before getting up properly, noticed the post on the floor but it was ages before I got around to it. When I finally did, there was a letter from the Prime Minister's Office telling me I'd been awarded the MBE for services to sport, broadcasting and charity. I wept to myself among the bills and junk mail. In the past I've been a bit blasé about honours, but all that changes. The letter stressed that the information was confidential for a month – breathe a word to a soul and I could be dragged off to the Tower. I blew it before the day was out. Told Nikki and my mum. It was as much as I could do, not to shout it from the rooftops.

I have to accept that I'm now better known for having cancer than I am for anything I did previously. It's an odd feeling.

'What do you do?'

'Oh I'm a cancer patient, but I do a little television on the side.'

The press coverage of my illness has been overwhelmingly positive, but it has portrayed me in the simplistic way that is the bread and butter of popular journalism. A reporter faced with writing an attention-grabbing piece in 500 words has no room for the nuances of human character. You are either hero or villain, winner or loser. One recent article described my media image as a cross between a Sherman tank and Mother Theresa. Neither of these are remotely me. I'm just an ordinary person learning to live as best I can with a body that has gone wrong, and with a strong belief that if I get my mind right, it can make quite a difference to my life expectancy.

There are times when I find the publicity very oppressive and I just want to be left alone to get on with what's left of my life. Some might say that, in telling my story and keeping myself so publicly high profile, I have sacrificed the right to privacy. I have to acknowledge that there is validity to this point of view, but I never set out to court publicity for my illness. I told my story initially to correct errors in the press coverage when I was first ill, and the whole thing snowballed from there. Going back to work fuelled it, but that was something I did for the benefit of my own health, mental attitude and need to earn a living, not for any reason of publicity.

I'm starting to sound defensive here. The fact is that, like it or not, publicity has surrounded my illness and I figured, that being the case, I might as well use it to help others. Hence the QED programme. Before the programme, I had become accustomed to lots of letters and people I didn't know stopping to say kind things to me. In the immediate aftermath of the broadcast the response was quite overwhelming. Nikki and I went shopping in Chelmsford the day after the programme went out. So many people thanked us for it and offered their support. It was quite amazing. Any cynical views I might have entertained about the 'I'm all right, Jack' attitude of the great British public evaporated for ever at that point.

So, too, have those old myths about typical British reserve. People I have never met have come up to me in the supermarket, put their arms around me and cried. Somebody stopped me in the High Street and offered a picture they had drawn of me, a very nice one as it happens. People stop to say, 'We have been praying for you this week and lit a candle in the church.' I find myself hugging complete strangers. I'm not normally a publicly demonstrative person, I'm no Mo Mowlem, so this has been a strangely out of character thing for me to do. But it's impossible not to respond spontaneously. It's as if I matter to them, as if I were a relative or close friend. On one occasion a London cab driver called Percy refused to take any money for my fare and just wanted to chat.

Of course, it's not unusual for people with familiar TV faces to get treated like acquaintances when they are going about their daily business. In a shop, restaurant or train somebody will greet you heartily and start to go through the normal social pleasantries. You can see in their eyes that they are struggling

Nobody was more surprised than me. Receiving the 1996 Sports Presenter of the Year Award.

You wouldn't have seen a line-up like this ten years ago. Female presenters for the BBC's Summer of Sport, 1996 – *(left to right)* Me, Sharron Davies, Sybil Ruscoe, Sue Barker and Hazel Irvine.

Bob, Megs and *(inset)* Anna Wilson at Bob's *This is Your Life*, November 1998.

Four of my lovely BBC colleagues – (*clockwise from top left*) Trevor Brooking, feet up with Michael Buerk, Huw Edwards and Peter Sissons.

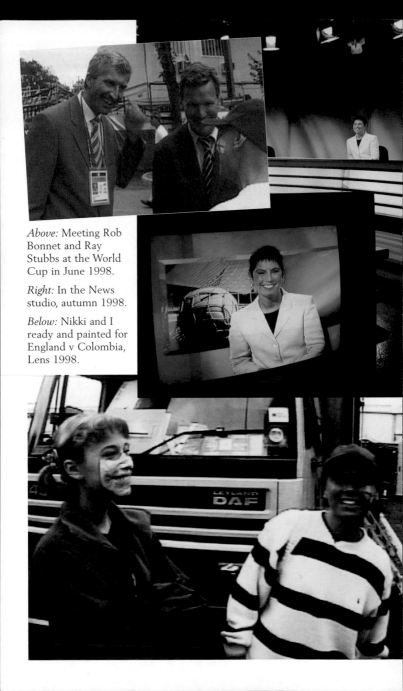

Above: Meeting Rob Bonnet and Ray Stubbs at the World Cup in June 1998.

Right: In the News studio, autumn 1998.

Below: Nikki and I ready and painted for England v Colombia, Lens 1998.

Above: Shivering in Lourdes, April 1998. (*Left to right*) Sue, Nikki, me and Deb.

Left: Dr Neville Davidson, my resolute oncologist.

Below: My painting of Padstow harbour featured in the *Holiday Heaven* programme, September 1998.

With Luke Wilson and Sam Gordon – brave kids fighting bone cancer and leukaemia. Child of Achievement Awards, February 1999.

Receiving my Pride of Britain Award from Cilla Black, May 1999.

Presenting the prizes in the 1999 London Women's Wheelchair Marathon with Tony Banks MP, Minister for Sport. (*Left to right*) me, Monica Wetterstrom (winner), Tony Banks and Tanni Grey (second).

Above: At Jim Old's stables with Des Lynam, Judith Hahn, John Motson and Out of the Deep, May 1999.

Left: Receiving my MBE from the Queen, July 1999.

Below: Horsy people – Alex Ferguson with his horse Queensland Star after a win at Newmarket.

In my garden, January 1999.

to remember who you are. 'Is she the cashier at the bank, or the woman from next door but one?' Sometimes the realisation dawns and the puzzlement turns to a look that says, 'What do you mean by jumping out of the television into real life.' But the encounters I have had recently haven't been like that. They have been with people who really wanted to say something to me as a person, to offer me their help. That's so humbling I almost don't know how to deal with it.

Then there have been the letters. If I'm not on the television, people write because they are worried, and if I am on there they write to say how nice it is to see me and how well I am looking. I try hard to reply to every letter I receive, but there are so many, it's very hard to keep on top of it. Even with the secretarial help that the Beeb has provided from time to time I'm struggling.

There are all manner of letters. So many of those who write are sweet and considerate. They include lines like, 'Please don't worry about replying, just concentrate on getting better.' But there are people who seem to feel that you have some sort of obligation towards them and want to enter into a protracted correspondence. It's almost as if they want a piece of you. I can't handle too much of that. It's enough of a struggle to keep my own body and soul together, without taking responsibility for the counselling and support of numerous others. From time to time I'll phone somebody who has written, but there is a limit to the number of times I can do that.

Some correspondents want to share their experiences of cancer and to tell me about the things that have worked for them. Others write long biographical letters – pages and pages about themselves – sharing the sort of information that would normally be reserved for close friends and relatives. At first this bothered me, but I came to realise that the act of writing these things could be therapeutic. Not surprising really, considering the task I'm currently engaged on.

And inevitably there are letters which are slightly nutty. One I received last week offered me a sort of tourist guide to heaven and a sure-fire method by which I could communicate with my nearest and dearest after I have departed. I guess I'll have to memorise the contents. Not much chance of taking it with me.

Some letters stand out as very special. I had one earlier this year from a woman who had watched the QED film and recognised what she thought were similar symptoms to mine. She went to the doctor and, sure enough, was diagnosed with cancer. So far pretty depressing, but here comes the amazing bit. The doctor told her that if she had left it just a few weeks longer, the disease would have progressed to a point where it was inoperable, but because it had been caught in time there was an excellent chance of recovery. That one letter justified the making of the programme for me. In my line of work it's not often you get the sense that something you have done may actually have saved someone's life.

There is a responsibility that comes with all this. Even though I know I'm not as brave and determined as I'm sometimes portrayed, I feel I've got to live up to what is expected of me. It's almost as if I would be letting people down if I didn't continue to pull out all the stops to keep myself going. I find that hard when I'm really unwell and my spirit saps, but I have to acknowledge that it acts as a spur, urging me to overcome the latest setbacks and difficulties. In the last few weeks the spur has not been quite so strong, perhaps because I'm so much more tired. And sometimes I just want to be left alone. That worries me because there is no doubt that people I have never met before have helped me a great deal along the way.

My relationship with the newspapers has been paradoxical. On the one hand they have been the source of some significant stress, but they have also provided me with some wonderful highs. Take the *Sun*, for example. They got hold of a copy of the QED tape a week before it was due to be broadcast and their pre-publicity led to me being hounded by all and sundry, which left me feeling a bit peed off. But I have to acknowledge that their coverage of me has been so positive that if I were to moan about them it would seem churlish in the extreme. Their readership was even good enough to vote me their woman of the year, and that was a tremendous honour. Other newspapers have been equally generous. The *Mirror* has recently launched its own appeal in support of my charity, and in only two weeks has raised £40,000.

That's where the paradox really lies. If I go along with the publicity, it can help to raise major sums of money for others and maybe assist some people to feel that they are not the only ones with this disease. At the same time, I'm bound to feel guilty because I'm aware that thousands of other cancer sufferers are getting on with their lives just as stoically, are being at least if not more brave than I am, and are doing it without the support that has come my way. It's an odd and rather uncomfortable feeling.

I've been to some pretty flash events, but the *Mirror* Pride of

Britain awards ceremony at the Dorchester has to be up at the top. So many really top-notch celebs there – Tony and Cherie Blair, Queen Noor of Jordan, Mick Hucknall, the Spice Girls, David Ginola and loads more. For me, the biggest thrill of all was meeting Sir Paul McCartney. Suddenly, there he was, and he had just said, 'Hello.'

I did a classic double take. Here was somebody out of my all-time list of top-ten heroes. As a child and teenager I was a major Beatles fan and even now, almost thirty years after they disbanded, I would still answer 'The Beatles' if asked to name my favourite group. I was a high-spirited eight-year-old in 1964 when they were at the very peak of their popularity, and I remember at that time going to stay at my cousin Jem's house. He was away, but his record player and collection of Beatles records were what particularly interested me. I played them over and over again, twisting and shouting myself into a happy frenzy. My favourite, 'Eight Days a Week', must have been almost worn through by the end of the trip.

At home, minus Beatles records, I had a special breakfast plate with the faces of all the Beatles on it. Food had to be strategically positioned – definitely no scrambled egg allowed on Paul McCartney's face. I was never a screaming, hysterical, Beatlemania type of fan. That sort of emotion wasn't encouraged in our family, and I had neither money nor opportunity to get to see them live. I simply bought the *Official Beatles Fan Club Magazine* and dreamt. In my teens when I finally got my own record player, I began to buy the records which had earlier passed me by.

Recently, Paul McCartney has had a different significance

for me, no less influential. Linda's fight against cancer, and his enormous dignity following her death, have moved me greatly. When he came up and spoke to me at the Pride of Britain Awards, I felt a great wave of affection for this man I adore, but don't know. He smiled, and held my hands. I was quite overwhelmed. It was so strange finally to meet my idol and feel these unexpected emotions. He rubbed my aching back as he chatted to me and I wanted to cry. He told me how much he missed 'his baby' and I could see in his beautiful eyes that sadness of bereavement still. She was a woman who rose above the huge and frequently hostile media pressure to make a brilliant success of marriage and motherhood, as well as carving a distinct and abiding role for herself. No typical showbiz wife this. It is so uplifting to hear of a showbiz couple who truly respect and love each other. Paul and Linda McCartney's life strikes me as one which was full of mutual admiration.

When the *Mirror* called me about the Pride of Britain Awards, I thought they were asking me to present one. I was shocked when they said I had been chosen to receive one. It was an honour to be in the company of the other award recipients, people more special than I could ever hope to be. I found myself reflecting on what courage is all about. These amazing people showed a combination of spontaneous bravery – risking everything to help someone else – and long-distance courage – refusal to give up, hanging in there against the odds.

Bravery of the spontaneous variety was shown by people such as bus driver Michael McNally who drove his bus into the immediate aftermath of the Omagh bombing to rescue dozens of badly injured survivors, despite the fact that a second device was being searched for. There were also the three volunteer lifeboatmen who put their lives on the line when they attempted to steer their sixteen-foot inflatable between jagged rocks in twenty-foot seas to rescue two people trapped in a cave. And there was fourteen-year-old Sarah Dinsdale who rescued her mother from a submerged car in a freezing river.

Those who refused to be beaten included Doreen and Neville Lawrence who have spent six years fighting to make sure that the facts behind their son Stephen's death were not swept under the carpet; and Donna McGillion who has fought her way back from the most horrendous injuries received in the Omagh blast. She said, 'I won't let the bombers destroy me, otherwise they will have won.'

Some combined both types of courage. Daniel Gallimore intervened to help somebody being attacked by a gang and was left so severely injured that he was in a coma for six weeks and on a life support system for ten. He had to endure a year in hospital, the loss of his eyesight, job, house and girlfriend. But he isn't bitter. He is rebuilding his life and working to help others.

I'm sure that none of these special people would say they were never afraid. But as somebody once said, 'Courage is not the absence of fear, but rather the judgement that something else is more important than fear.' I'm sure, too, that none would say that they chose to be in the position they found themselves. There's this myth that the world is made up of brave people and cowardly people, and that the brave ones are just sticking around waiting for something brave to do. In fact, real bravery is something that only emerges in the unexpected events and the shitty twists of life, and it often surprises the very people who display it.

So can we all be brave? Yes, I think we probably can. But like so much in life there is an element to it which is about habit. If you turn away from challenge or give up in the face of adversity once, it's so much easier to do the same again the next time, and the next. Showing some courage in minor difficulties is probably good training for the major crises. There's a wonderful line with a sporting feel that sums this up for me: 'Courage is like a muscle. It is strengthened with use.'

12

A Voyage of Discovery

I N the early months of my illness, I did a great deal of praying. I've never been a particularly religious person, but I think I believed in God at that time. I was helped by a wonderful chaplain, Reverend Stephen Henwood, from the St. Francis Hospice who visited me, talked and prayed with me. He was probably the first vicar with whom I've felt totally comfortable.

Terminal illness must inevitably cause you to examine your beliefs and for many it leads to a strengthening of faith. That's what happened for me in the early stages. But it all evaporated very suddenly in the spring of 1998, around the time of the failed liver operation. After months of hope and effort I was totally knocked back and I became very angry. I can even pinpoint the day when I said to myself, 'I no longer believe in God.' It was 11th April. A colleague had organised a day trip to Old Trafford for Nikki and myself to watch a Manchester United game. It was a trip that Nikki had been looking forward to for ages and I was keen that it should be special for her. The weather and traffic on the way were utterly horrendous and we got so badly delayed that we missed more than half of the match. Seven hours to get there and another five to get back. We could hear the game over the radio while we were sitting in a traffic jam.

Now what was it about that incident that finally broke my remaining faith? I don't know. Probably it was all about straws and camels, something that had been building up in me over the weeks and snapped at that point. It was as if I was saying, 'Look, I don't ask much, but if you can't help Nikki with a day out that means so much to her, what can I expect of you?'

I can almost hear some readers tut-tutting. 'With all the suffering in the world, you expect God to be concerned about you getting to a football match on time?' Well, yes. It seems ridiculously trivial and selfish when I write it down, but after all the bad deals of the previous months, I felt we really deserved a break at that time. And as I say, the match was just a catalyst.

Actually, Nikki was great about the trip. She said she had really enjoyed herself. But I steamed about it for days.

I haven't recovered that lost belief. Stephen Henwood has continued to visit me. I tell him I don't believe in it anymore, and he's very patient. He doesn't worry about that at all. Chats and prayers with him are still comforting. And it's not that I don't want to believe – it just went, that's all. For all that, the letters I get from people who do believe touch me greatly. When people tell me that they are praying for me, or that they have all lit candles for me in the church that day, I think, 'How amazing – that's very special.' Just because I'm not particularly religious, it doesn't mean that I think any less of those kind of acts.

I haven't lost my belief in some kind of supernatural force.

I don't know quite what it is. There have been several times when I have felt that I'm being looked after in some way by what I call my force, my energy, my help. I struggle to articulate it. Every now and again when things are bad I turn to this force, whatever it is, to say, 'Please help me' or 'I'm sure you won't be able to sort this out because I've caught you at a bad moment.' When things are good I also say thank you, grateful for the fact that I've just gone through an experience which is a nice one. But it's a belief which ebbs and flows. When I'm very poorly I don't believe this force exists at all.

Somebody suggested to me that the force I described sounded like God in plain clothes, but it's not like that. It's just something being around that gives me a helping hand. It isn't a person so much as an energy – a connection between all living things – and something individuals can connect with.

I'm conscious that this is not terribly coherent, and I apologise for that. But it's not some carefully worked out philosophy, just my response to life and my situation.

How come I continue to derive so much comfort from spiritual healing? Well, in a way, it doesn't matter if you don't entirely subscribe to the detail. I don't believe in God and angels in the way that Laura the healer does, but I can relate her explanation to my notion of a universal energy. She says that I'm being helped by all the people praying for me and, yes, I can believe that, even if I can't quite believe in the entity to whom they are praying.

For a while I think I did believe in life after death. Nobody in my circle of friends and relatives had died for a number of years, and then in the last year, seven people whom I know well have gone. I started to get the morbid notion that perhaps they were paving the way for me – you know, a sort of family to go to. I looked for some sign they were there, but of course I didn't get it. Really, it was just a bit of fantasy thinking. It would be nice to believe it, but I can't.

And what if I'm wrong, and there is a life after death?

Well, that will be a nice surprise.

The prospect of dying no longer arouses the same fear in me that it did when I was first diagnosed. I've been setting myself this goal of seeing Nikki through her GCSEs and I'm no longer desperately worried if I go as soon as she has had her results. Those other longer term goals I had, like making it to the Sydney 2000 Olympics, are starting to look very shaky and I don't mention them anymore. Things have got so much worse in the last few weeks. As I've said before, it is the vision of the aftermath in terms of Nikki and others which is the greatest source of distress. If only I could do something about removing her fear, then I think I could feel content that we had done it all, and I'd be quite happy to go. I'm not afraid of it, and there are too many days that are not great days, when the pain takes over from everything else. These are the days when you want to close your eyes and not wake up.

But I'm not ready to go yet. I want to do the things I've said I'll do. As ever, I hate letting people down, and death does feel like the ultimate let down. I can't quite bring myself to stop saying, 'Hey, we can turn this around' either. I know I'm on the downward slope, I am prepared for death, but I want it to be on my terms. I still hate to think of this wretched disease sneaking up and carrying me away when I'm not ready for it.

The media world I work in is quite a small one and it's a lot more caring than outsiders might imagine. People get to know each other well and the loss of a colleague hits people hard. The death of Jill Dando earlier this year was traumatic for everyone in broadcasting. Like everyone else, I was horrified by the news. The death of somebody you know and like a lot is always difficult to handle, but when it comes so suddenly and violently it leaves you in a state of shock.

Once I had come to terms with the fact of Jill's death, I couldn't help but compare what happened to her with my own situation. If you are going to die young, or at any age for that matter, is it better to go suddenly like that, without any warning in the middle of a normal day, or to have months to prepare for death in the way that I have? I think that having the time to prepare has to be preferable. People are always appalled at the idea of being given three months, six months or a year to live, but it does have its benefits. Like it or not, the death sentence is there hanging over all of us from the day we are born, but most of the time we manage to avoid thinking about it.

A terminal diagnosis changes that. It gives you the time to address the things that are really important to you and to get yourself sorted in advance of the inevitable. In many ways it's like winning the lottery. It's not a particularly good lottery – you could call it the bum lottery – but like the other sort it frees you up to do whatever you want. I don't mean that in a material sense, obviously there are financial and family constraints in all our lives, but there is a definite psychological opening up of possibilities. You're no longer constrained in the way you were before. People cannot begrudge you the freedom to deal with your remaining months as you would wish.

There are some cancer patients who act as if they really have won the lottery and go into a self-indulgent lifestyle aimed entirely at self-preservation. Three months in a San Diego clinic, for example. I've read one or two books by such people and haven't been that impressed. Doesn't seem to have done too much for them. Quite apart from the fact that in my situation it's not something I could contemplate, I'm far from convinced it's the right thing to do. It's a bit like those people who retire, sell up and buy their dream cottage in the country or villa in Spain, only to find that they've cut themselves off from everything that previously gave their lives meaning. Attractive though the thought may be, and even if I could afford it, three months stewing in a luxury clinic would leave me adrift from the people and activities that provide the buzz and sparkle to my life.

That isn't to say that I haven't grabbed the opportunities for a bit of self-indulgence. I have done so many wonderful things in the last two years, met so many remarkable people and been given so many opportunities that I would never have experienced if I had remained well. Without the cancer, I would still be bashing away on Breakfast television and knackering myself. But all these wonderful experiences have been within the context of my normal life, with people I know and love.

People write to me and say, 'I see you on television, you look great. What are you doing that I'm not?'

Probably not much, is the answer. I have to tell them that there is no miracle potion. The treatments I'm having are much the same as anyone else. I'm taking vitamins, but don't necessarily believe in them. I'm trying to maintain a diet, but don't necessarily believe in it. I'm taking Chinese herbs, but don't necessarily believe in them. At times I would like to stop all of them just to see what happens. If I'm lucky I have two or three good days a week, but I have managed to gear myself up for the days when I'm due to work, and that's when the viewer sees me.

I know that to some people that sort of answer is a bit of a disappointment. They would like to feel that there is something they haven't heard of yet, some medicine, food or therapy that would get them through it. At the end of the twentieth century we're victims of the success of medical science – so used to the wonder drug and the miracle surgery that when faced with a condition that medicine cannot hack, we can't quite believe it.

I need to remind people, too, about the advanced stage my cancer had reached at the time it was discovered, and the fact that all our bodies are different. The treatments and therapies I have followed may not have done the trick for me, but that doesn't mean that they won't work for somebody else.

So, I've not found a miracle potion, but I have found some other valuable things. At the start of this book I likened life since diagnosis to a voyage of discovery. I guess the voyage was a bit like Dorothy's trip to Oz. I find myself, at the end of it, concluding that many of the most important things I sought were there all the time. I just needed to realise that they were there and were applicable to my situation, or to have them pointed out to me.

Whatever the challenge – cancer, bereavement, physical struggle – some of the most valuable resources for tackling it are inside you. There are all manner of external things that can help a cancer patient – treatments, caring medical staff, supportive friends and family – but without the ingredient you put in yourself, you are really going to struggle. I certainly don't know it all, but I do know that four or five simple things about my own approach have helped to keep me going.

The first of these is the use of achievable goals to help me deal with the biggest challenge of my life. I've always set myself goals, but I've never needed them more, and I've never needed to give so much attention to making them graduated. The technique is one which will be familiar to anyone who has participated in endurance sports or tough physical challenges. Say, for example, that you are proposing to swim the Channel, climb a mountain or complete a triathlon. Looking at the challenge as a whole is daunting – the pain, the slog, the exhaustion. But break down that ultimate goal into bite-sized pieces and it becomes achievable – covering the next mile, getting to the next rock, even taking the next step. Frank Dick gave me a nice little line for it: 'Life by the yard is apt to be hard. Life by the inch is a bit of a cinch.' Tackled this way you can do it. What works for sport and adventure works for cancer. Without these goals, milestones, call them what you will, you run the risk that the whole thing will overwhelm you.

So I set my goals all the time, and each one takes me a bit further up the mountain. Some are just single steps – making it through the day with a sense of achievement. Others are slightly further away – Nikki's GCSEs, the next holiday. It's important to have these longer term targets, too. They serve to measure progress in ways that the single steps can't.

You don't just need something to aim for, you need firm ground under you feet while you are getting there. Remember the story Terry Moule told me about the dragon – people falling off the path because of all the loose stones. There are several ways I try to make sure I don't slip or fall. They don't always work – you will have realised that in the course of this book – but they work more often than not.

I actively seek out the positive. It's not just a matter of being a positive character. I have to work on it when things are grim. I look for any one thing that I can build on to turn the situation around. Usually I can find something. I look back over previous struggles where I've managed to succeed, and I tell myself that if I could get through that, then I can certainly hack whatever the latest problem might be. I seek out my heroes – I've described some of them in the book, people who have overcome far greater obstacles than mine – and I draw strength and inspiration from them.

I invest in hope. By this I mean that I try to bank the positive vibes with others around me. It's partly that I don't like making other people miserable, but I also know that my mood can affect the outlook of others, which may in turn make me more pessimistic. If I'm able to emphasise the positive, they will find it easier to boost me when I'm down. It's not about fooling myself or others, just recognising the importance of mutual support.

So that's the targets sorted and the firm ground under your feet while you are getting there. What else?

211

Well, the next thing has to be about keeping going. My obsession about not giving up may appear like stubbornness in the face of the inevitable, but as I've already said, the inevitable is there for all of us. I believe that we can influence when it is going to happen. I've always taken pride in not being a quitter, and sometimes that's been to my detriment, but I've learned through this illness that you have to keep on going because you never know when the breaks are going to come.

A couple of years ago I was fascinated and inspired by the story of Tony Bullimore. He was the lone yachtsman whose boat the *Exide Challenger* lost its keel and capsized in mountainous seas during the 1997 Vendee Global Challenge. Tony spent nearly five days under the partly submerged hull of his boat 1500 miles south of Australia in the freezing waters of the Southern Ocean before, through an incredible stroke of luck, he was spotted and rescued by an Australian Navy frigate. Any reasonable assessment of the situation would conclude that it was impossible to survive a shipwreck in those conditions for so long, and indeed the searchers had shifted their emphasis from rescue to recovery of a body. Death seemed inevitable, but Tony Bullimore kept himself alive in what he described as his washing machine from hell, saying to himself, 'Keep going. Never give up.' After he was rescued, his wife was quoted as saying, 'Tony is stubborn. If he makes up his mind to do something, he'll do it.'

I'm not seeking to compare my situation with his – goodness knows, I am completely in awe of bravery like that. But I do recognise his way of thinking. If you're not a quitter, you don't become one just because the odds get tougher. You do the best you can with what you're dealt.

The final ingredient in my personal survival recipe has to be an ability to seize the day.

Friends reading this will say, 'Oh, yes, I wondered when that was going to come up.' It has been my motto for a long time. But never has it been more important to me than over the past two years. Living with cancer has taught me a lot about using that most precious resource – time. I've learned to recognise what is important in my life and spend time on those things, and I've learned to take nothing for granted. I have learned about living in the present and using my available energy to get in as much happiness as possible. I make a determined effort not to waste that energy asking why I should have found myself in such a pickle, and I don't fritter away the good times agonising about what might go wrong in the future. Whoever you are, whatever your circumstances – life's too short for any of that.

There's an old Zen parable which says it better than I can. It goes like this.

A man was walking through the woods when suddenly a large tiger jumped out and started to chase him. He fled to the edge of a precipice and, grabbing hold of a vine, he swung himself over the edge and out of the reach of the tiger. As he hung there he could hear the tiger pawing the ground and growling. And then he heard another sound, a small chomping. Looking up he saw that a mouse was nibbling its way through the vine from which he was hanging. He looked down, and far below him he could see another tiger

213

prowling around waiting to eat him if he fell. Just then he noticed a ripe strawberry right next to his hand. He picked it and ate it.

The strawberry tasted delicious!

13

May to July 1999

I T's now the end of July, and the last few weeks have been the toughest yet.

In late May, things started to go seriously awry. The pain in my liver was awful. It felt grazed and bruised. A CT scan revealed that the tumours were breaking through the membrane that surrounds the liver – no wonder I was in so much pain. Pretty depressing. I was aware that this was something associated with the latter stages of liver cancer, and began to wonder how much longer I could last.

Further changes to my treatment were needed. I had my first hit of radiotherapy. After so many different treatments – over fifty sessions of chemotherapy – here I was having radiotherapy for the first time. It lasted just seven minutes, three and a half minutes each side – the same as for a rare steak, I believe. For all the horror stories about radiotherapy, I found it a lot less hassle than chemo and experienced none of the nausea I had been led to expect.

As I waited for a clever scan which would pinpoint exactly where the radiotherapy needed to be directed, I sat next to a lady who seemed so much weaker and sicker than me. It made me realise how relatively healthy and privileged I was, and I resolved not to feel so sorry for myself. Later an old man in the waiting room described his lung operation for me in gruesome detail, and I started feeling sorry for myself again. I had an injection to raise the white blood cell count and a couple of blood transfusions. They seemed to help, as did the increased emphasis on pain control.

I got home feeling very poorly and in a lot of pain. Nikki caught me in this low state and it upset her. Luckily, after food and painkillers, I started to feel much better and was able to convince both of us that this was a temporary blip. Just as well. The last thing she needed with six GCSEs in the next three days was worrying about me on the downward slope.

Work was a struggle. It was an increasing effort to get myself up for the Friday sports review, and additional interviews were really taking it out of me. Even getting dressed was becoming a problem. On the weekend of 19th June I was due to present the Friday sports review, and to anchor the European Cup athletics on the Sunday. I managed the Friday session, but I was in real pain and very dopey from the painkillers. I actually slept in the Sports room for most of the afternoon and only went down to the Newsroom just before the bulletin. Peter Sissons was there, and he greeted me in the lovely way he always does. He gave me a hug. 'Ow!' It was so painful that I cried. Comes to something, doesn't it, when one of the most comforting things possible makes you blub.

I just about managed to get through the bulletin, but I had to draw on every last ounce of my resources. I felt relieved but tearful afterwards, and knew there was no way I could even contemplate doing the athletics later that weekend. The following day I was whipped into hospital and was so whacked I simply slept all day. When I was awake it seemed as if I was in a dream, I had double vision and most worrying of all was the fact that my memory seemed to have gone. It was all very very scary.

I remained in hospital for the next three weeks. More blood transfusions, nerve block and a Hickman line. That's a line directly into a fast-flowing blood vessel near to the heart, that allows injections and treatments to be administered in the most efficient way possible. Chemo infusion was discussed, but I wasn't strong enough for it. The tiredness was uncontrollable, the effects of the drugs, I assume. I would drift in and out of sleep at the drop of a hat. Sometimes it was in the middle of a conversation, which was most disconcerting.

I lost time and very nearly lost my life. Came within an inch of it. Somehow though, I wasn't ready to go. On at least two occasions the doctors didn't think I would live another day, and frankly, neither did I. But somehow I did. By 10th July my condition was stable enough for me to be allowed home. But it was a grim homecoming. The emphasis was on ensuring as comfortable an end as possible. That Saturday the doctors told me that I had only days to live, possibly no more than three.

Three days took me to 13th July, the day before I was due to receive the MBE at the Palace. Whatever else I did, I wanted to be there. I set about conserving my energy so that I could make the trip. Not easy to do. There were calls and visits from friends desperately concerned about me, and conversations took on the form of goodbyes.

I made it to the Wednesday with enough life in me to go for it. Arrival at the Palace was scheduled for 10.15 and that meant getting up at six o'clock to be ready for a car at eight. I was panicking about whether we would get there. Nothing to do with my health, just concern about the London traffic. Getting into clothes was a major effort. My mother, sister and Nikki were due to come with me, and it had been agreed that a doctor from the hospital would accompany us to sort me out medically if necessary. At eight sharp we were waved off by neighbours. I spent the whole journey fretting about the traffic, and it must have been an immense relief to everyone else when we rolled through the gates of Buck House at 10.15 on the dot. After the anxiety of the journey, I had to take a few minutes to calm down.

A footman was at the car door almost before it had stopped. 'Miss Rollason. Lovely to see you.'

He put me in a wheelchair – no royal crests on it, what a disappointment – and whisked me through a back route to where there was a lift. Now I'd like to be able to tell you that this unconventional entrance gave me a unique insight into behind-the-scenes life at the Palace – corgis enjoying Pedigree Chum from the finest porcelain, the Queen's copy of the *Sun* being ironed in readiness for her royal perusal – but, alas, I can't. All I saw were some corridors and the inside of a lift.

My family were ushered away to join the ranks of other accompanying guests, and the doctor and I waited in line for the big moment. I was pleased to see my friend Stephanie

Moore there. Stephanie is the widow of the late Bobby Moore and she was also receiving the MBE for her work with cancer charities. Bobby Moore, incidentally, had almost exactly the same problem as me, and Stephanie has been tremendously supportive to me over the last couple of years.

The Queen came down from the dais to present my MBE. Not much chance of me being able to get up there. She chatted to me about my time in broadcasting, and then, really sweet, said how thrilled she was to be able to give me the award.

'Not half as thrilled as I am to receive it, Your Majesty.'

No, I didn't say that. In fact I'm not sure what I did say. I got confused about when to say Ma'am and when to say Your Majesty, and came away convinced that I'd said the wrong thing. But I suppose most people do that. She must be pretty used to it.

I rejoined my family after the presentation and shared perceptions of the event. Nikki said she had rather expected the Queen to be bigger and more regal. My mother complained that she was only able to see the top of the Queen's head. I'm not sure whether this is a common source of disappointment, but if it is, royal watchers must be pleased to see how tall Prince William has become.

We arrived home about three and enjoyed a gentle celebration late lunch with friends and neighbours. It wasn't quite the way I had hoped to receive the award but, boy, was I pleased to have made it.

In the last few days I've had some hugely encouraging calls and visits. David Coleman has been on the phone telling me to keep on fighting. Des and Motty, too, and the crowd from

BBC News have called me regularly as well. The other day Frank Dick arrived. He had the Essex and England cricketer, Ronnie Irani in tow. Talk about not wanting to put us to any trouble, Ronnie had even brought his own sandwiches. He's so much larger than life and kept us thoroughly amused.

Today is a good day. I'm feeling so much better than I was. Right now I should be receiving an honorary doctorate at Brighton University, but even the way I feel today, a journey down to the south coast would be out of the question. So instead of me going there to receive it, Paul Griffiths, Dean of the Education Faculty, came to my house last week to present it to me. We made an occasion of it, friends and family, about twenty of us – slightly fewer than the 800 who will be at today's graduation ceremony. Paul Griffiths was all set to hand me the degree, when we asked him to make the speech that he would have made at the ceremony. Here in my living room, he made a lovely speech and then presented the doctorate to tumultuous applause. Well, as tumultuous as you can get with twenty people.

It's amusing to think that in the last couple of weeks I've gone from plain Helen Rollason to Dr Helen Rollason MBE. I guess you could call me a late developer.

For a while after coming out of hospital I felt as if I wasn't here. There were so many people rallying round to help, and for all that I knew I needed them and appreciated what they were doing, there were times when I wanted to be able to tell them all to go. It was that independence thing again. I had an agency nurse full time, my sister, Nikki and neighbours doing all they could.

Ali has been quite brilliant, not only in assisting me, but in fielding phone calls and helping visitors to feel at ease when they arrive not knowing what to expect. Hazel has devoted so much love and attention to me, and other neighbours have delighted me with their gestures of affection. Today some tinkling wind chimes and a beautiful tub of flowers appeared, as if by magic, on the front porch.

For all that, I have needed to prove I can still do things for myself. We've dispensed with the services of the nurse and I'm being allowed to administer the drugs and even to look after the various cancer treatments myself. I've had a haircut, managed to shave my legs, and it feels as if I've started to move into the present tense. I'm pushing towards going to Cornwall in mid-August. Everybody thought I was mad when I first suggested it, but I think they now realise how important it is for me to have a goal to work towards.

Postscript

SADLY, Helen didn't make the trip to Cornwall, but that goal was no less important for not being achieved. It was something else to visualise and to work towards during those final weeks.

My last meeting with Helen was on 30th July, just over a week before her death. It was she who came to the door when I knocked, cordless phone to her ear and busily engaged in conversation. She was weak, and behind her eyes the suffering of the previous few weeks, but she was bright and alert. As ever, she asked after me and my family before permitting any questions about herself. I had arrived, knowing how ill she was, and with no expectation of working on her book. 'I'm just visiting,' I stressed.

I should have known better. She briskly pushed aside my concerns about her health and insisted that we did some serious work. It was one of the hottest days of the year and we sat in the shade of the garden as she recounted the events of the couple of weeks just past – her visit to the Palace, presentation of the honorary doctorate, the way she had come back from the brink yet again. We also chatted about her plans for the trip to Cornwall later in August and dealt with some gaps in earlier parts of the book.

As she talked I watched her brighten and grow. The inimitable grin came more readily, and her natural sparkle overcame the exhaustion in her eyes. This was Helen doing what she enjoyed most – communicating, creating something, and having a good laugh in the process. So immersed were we, that it came as a shock to both of us when rumbling tummies and slanting sun signalled evening, and we realised that we had been talking for four and a half hours.

It was easily the most special of all the sessions we had working on this book. We had talked frankly about death weeks before, and had exchanged what we thought were goodbyes two weeks previously when Helen was not expected to survive more than a few days. There were no painful or difficult things left unsaid and that helped to make it a magical afternoon for both of us.

Over the next few days Helen weakened markedly and spent a lot of time sleeping, but there was no way that she was going to be confined to bed. She spent the greater part of every day dressed and downstairs and was able to get out into the garden right up to Friday 6th August. When Keith Morton visited on the Tuesday, she asked him to provide her with a set of exercises that would help her get up and down the stairs. Only on the Sunday was she unable to get out of bed. She died peacefully on the morning of Monday 9th August with her family around her.

Helen's most important goal in recent months was to see

Nikki through her GCSEs and to be there when the results came through. She didn't make it to results day, but newspaper reports that she had sought a special dispensation from the exam boards to release the results early were inaccurate. Helen was insistent that there should be no special treatment. However, when it became clear that the end was near, teachers from Nikki's school came up with an estimate of the results based on their experience and knowledge of Nikki's course work, and passed it to the family in case it should be needed. And so it was that on the Friday before she died, after lunch in the garden with Nikki and ex-husband John, Helen opened the envelope and shared in her daughter's success

And how accurate was the estimate? Pretty close. Nikki achieved six A star grades, four A grades and one B.

Helen was a very special person to all who knew her and many who didn't. Part of that was down to her generosity about others' achievements and her modesty about her own. This book would not be complete without an appreciation of Helen's lasting contribution to sports broadcasting, disability sport, and cancer awareness, and some testimony to the love and affection so many people had for her.

So, quite without her permission, that is what follows.

John Caunt
August 1999

Rob Bonnet's Address to the Congregation at the Thanksgiving Service for Helen's Life

17th August, St Mary's Church, Shenfield

So there we were on the twelfth green at Royal Mid-Surrey – Bonnet and Sue Thearle versus Neil Bennett and Helen in a mixed fourball – friendly, up to that point. It's all-square. Rollas needs a tricky two and half foot putt to halve the hole and keep the match level.

Golfers amongst you will recognise this as an interesting moment, but if you don't know the complexities of a game that Helen loved, like most sports, then suffice it to say that things are getting tense.

Rollas looks enquiringly at me as if I might concede the putt – let her off the hook – but I only see her out of the corner of my eye because I'm suddenly taking an excessive interest in the pattern on the grip of my putter.

'Let's see what she's made of,' I'm thinking to myself.

As if Helen Rollason hadn't been used to having her ability challenged, her determination questioned, her character tested. And as if it wasn't going to happen time and time and time again in the future.

I'm still looking at my putter when I hear the sound of the

ball rattling in the cup. I look up to see that famous smile, perkier than ever. 'All square then, Bonny,' she says. Sheepish grin from Bonnet, his psychological strategy in tatters. Jaunty walk from Rollason to the next tee from where she and Neil impose themselves and go on to win by at least three holes, I think.

I say jaunty walk, but that's not quite true. This was a hot midsummer's day in 1997, a month, maybe two, before that dreadful morning when Nick Dickson and I fielded a call from Helen in the *Breakfast News* office. She was ringing in to say that she had cancer and that she wouldn't be coming to work for a while. Nick and I tried to absorb the full impact of what we'd been told. I know I couldn't.

And yet my mind went back to the Royal Mid-Surrey and to the memory of how, in retrospect, she'd dragged her feet perhaps a little from tee to green. By then, she'd been ill for a year, perhaps longer. Ahead of her at that point, two more years of fighting the disease that finally overwhelmed her. Two years in which all of us who knew and loved Helen recognised even more keenly why we felt the way we did.

To be told that you have merely a matter of months to live might make cowards of us all. Bitterness, self-defeat and self-pity might cause us to close our lives down. But that wasn't Helen Rollason. Instead, somehow, her life opened up in a way that was truly inspirational.

This wasn't just about defying the cautious predictions of the doctors and nurses who were to care so tenderly for her. It was about her forthright, feisty, no-nonsense hunger for understanding. It was about her love for her family, her daughter

Nikki especially, and it was about her enormous willpower, grit and courage. She disliked the tabloid cliché, 'Brave Helen'. So do I, but for different reasons. It doesn't do her justice. It must have taken exceptional strength of character to have lived that very same generous life of mischievous humour and genuine interest in those around her when she was so fully entitled to be morbid and self-centred.

Her closest friends all say the same thing – that she would always ask after them and their families before they could ask about her. She wasn't just avoiding the tricky questions, she simply had this unerring way of putting others first, even in her darkest moments. Beneficiaries from her own cancer charity will know that to be true, disabled sportsmen and women know it because of the work she did to promote the Paralympic movement, and the public at large know it because of *Hope for Helen*, that wonderful BBC1 film we all remember for its simple honesty and truth.

But she was, of course, no saint. In fact, she could be delightfully wicked. Deb Crook, who first met her as an eleven-year-old, told me that she was 'very naughty' at Bath High School for Girls, where she learned to 'run with the fox and hunt with the hounds'.

And I always sensed we were just a moment away from what would have been a major BBC incident every time Helen presented the Saturday sports news just before *Match of the Day*. 'If you don't want to know the results,' she'd say with that smile, 'then look away now.' You might have looked away, but I always suspected the devil in her was itching to tell you the results anyway once you'd looked back. It's a lovely fantasy but perhaps her friendship with Des would have suffered.

Laughter was at the very centre of her life. It was never cruel, and it was often self-deprecating. Many of you will have received her 1997 Christmas card, Santa Claus as a slaphead, an ironic reference to her loss of hair through chemotherapy. She went to Lourdes in France on the basis that she'd try anything, but once there, she dissolved in helpless mirth amidst the solemnity of a torchlit religious procession. The sisters weren't amused it seems. Even in the search for a miracle cure, Helen remained buoyant and irreverent.

She told me during a gossipy lunch in April that she wasn't afraid of dying. 'Giving up,' she'd famously said, 'just wasn't an option.' But by now the ups were less frequent and less meaningful than the downs. She hadn't given up – goodness knows, there were Nikki's GCSEs, a new role on the *Six o'Clock News* and, although she didn't know it at the time, an MBE to live for – but outwardly at least, she exuded a sense of reconciliation, a feeling that targets had been met or were about to be met and that there was an order and provision for what would follow.

We know the rest, the pain, the suffering, and the bravery. All of it part of her last appearance on the *Six* some two months ago. Those working with her saw her in great distress, but her performance betrayed none of this to the viewers who continued to write to her in their hundreds. Helen was genuinely astonished by the weight of the weekly postbag, and of course she felt awkward when personal replies became impossible.

We also know of the support and comfort she had towards the end from her closest friends, her family, and of course from Nikki herself. Our hearts go out to them today.

So how do we remember Helen Rollason? The facts are that she broke new ground for women in sports broadcasting, she raised the profile of sport for the disabled, she worked tirelessly when she was most tired for fellow cancer sufferers, and only last month, she went up to London to see the Queen. That was the ultimate recognition that Helen Rollason MBE had truly made a difference.

But if it's her humanity, not her biography that you want, then you'll simply hear her laughter and see her smile.

Rob Bonnet

Helen Rollason,
True Champion of Women's Sport

A tribute by Eleanor Oldroyd

In the annual calendar of events which make up the sports presenter's life, judging *The Sunday Times* Sportswomen of the Year Awards is not the most arduous task. You get to celebrate the achievements of the country's finest female competitors, to engage in passionate, sometimes heated, debate with like-minded colleagues about your favoured candidates and, not least, to enjoy a lavish and boozy lunch provided by our sponsors, Moët & Chandon.

It is one of the highlights of the year for me, as it was for my friend Helen Rollason, a true champion of women's sport. Two years ago, under the sook of the early stages of chemotherapy, and wearing one of her hated wigs, she arrived at the judges' lunch ready to do battle. Together we forged a vocal alliance to persuade our fellow judges round to our way of thinking – using purely democratic methods, of course. Afterwards, as most of us dived into rich sauces and puddings, Helen munched on the rather more abstemious menu approved by her doctors, and bemoaned not being able to share in a glass or two of our sponsors' finest.

By last year, she was having Good Days and Bad Days, and the judges' lunch fell on a Bad Day. Helen didn't feel up to the long drive from her home in Essex to Moët HQ in London. Nevertheless, she faxed us her thoughts on all the candidates, and after we had drawn up our shortlists in the various categories, it fell to me as chairwoman to phone Helen for her views. They were, as always, wise and trenchant, and in a couple of cases caused us to rethink our choices.

The awards ceremony a few weeks later was on a Good Day, and Helen was in fine form at lunch; discussing plans to compete in the Great North Run the following year, wondering who might sponsor her for MCC membership (current waiting list eighteen years). She never stopped setting herself targets. In a year when we had introduced a new category – for Inspiration – Helen could have won it hands down, had she been eligible. Many of the sportswomen who met her that day at the Gibson Hall commented on how her presence had lifted their spirits.

But then Helen had the power to inspire long before she contracted the awful illness which finally claimed her. Her fight against cancer was well documented, and may be what most people will remember her for; but she had already won some significant battles in her career.

When she became the first woman to present *Grandstand* on the BBC in 1990, she faced opposition and scepticism, and not necessarily from the audience. Some colleagues at the time were less than supportive; years later, she admitted having had the stuffing knocked out of her several times. As attitudes towards women in the business improved, and her professionalism, natural ability and deep sporting knowledge became better appreciated, life became easier; but Helen never stopped fighting. Even when the cancer and the chemotherapy were doing their worst, she kept badgering BBC Sport to give her things to do; presenting live athletics, travelling to Italy for a documentary on women football commentators. I am sure these workaholic tendencies helped to prolong her life.

She badgered me, too, in the nicest possible way. Always a champion of women colleagues whose professional abilities she respected (while crisply dismissive of the so called 'bimbo factor'), she cared deeply about equal opportunities in the world of sports presenting. The last time I saw her, in the BBC sportsroom in early June, she told me it was time I got myself back introducing the morning sports bulletins on BBC *Breakfast News*. So it was I found myself cueing into her obituary, and interviewing former colleague and close friend, Bob Wilson, on BBC1 the morning after her death. It was an emotional occasion, but I found myself buoyed by thoughts of Helen's incredible determination to overcome barriers, and not just the physical ones of her last months, but the psychological ones of her early career.

The last decade has seen women storming locations in TV sport which would have once seemed insurmountable. And much of that is due to Helen Rollason battering away at their foundations. The current generation of lipstick-wearing sports broadcasters have much to thank her for.

Eleanor Oldroyd

Helen's Contribution to Disability Sport

A tribute by Ian Hayden MBE,
President of Disability Sport England and
Paralympic Gold Medallist

I dedicate this tribute to Helen on behalf of all sportsmen and sportswomen with a disability because she championed us all; the grassroots through her support as a Vice Patron of Disability Sport England (formerly BSAD) and the élite by the positive way in which she always portrayed us as sports people first and foremost, whether reporting on our sport or in general conversation.

Helen had that rare ability of being able to influence people and alter their attitudes without them being aware that it was happening. Her strength of character, will and quiet determination were admired by all with whom she came into contact; as was her quick wit and humour which she used to overcome many a difficult situation. The media and sports world will remember the ground-breaking contribution that Helen made by her thoroughly professional approach and genuine commitment. Nowhere was this more evident than in her recognition of and respect for sportsmen and sportswomen with a disability.

Whilst pressing our cause for recognition as people seriously training and competing in sport, Helen also encouraged and advised us, as sports people and administrators, of what we needed to do to support and reinforce the effort being put in on our behalf.

Helen's genuine wish that sport for disabled people should receive its rightful recognition was well known. She did a fantastic job of carrying forward to new heights the momentum begun by Cliff Morgan, over some twenty years, and Ron Pickering – God bless them. There is no doubt that her enthusiasm influenced not only other sports commentators, but also the BBC in the improved coverage of our sport, particularly the Barcelona and Atlanta Paralympic Games.

As Vice Patron of Disability Sport England, Helen supported all our members at every opportunity and, with colleague Paul Dickinson, actively encouraged the media as a whole to give sportsmen and sportswomen with a disability more coverage at a local level.

I would like to conclude this tribute to Helen by asking her friends, particularly those in the media, to ensure that the commitment this special lady made to improving the quality of life for so many people will be continued in her memory.

Ian Hayden MBE

A Few of the
Many Other Tributes to Helen

'In her professional life, Helen was always incredibly sensitive to the highs and lows of sportsmen and women and they responded to her sensitivity. It was a quality she carried through to everyone she talked to.'

BOB WILSON

'Working with Helen, sitting next to her under studio pressure while she was fighting her illness, was an experience that will never leave me. The smile never grew dim, and only at the last did the strength begin to fade. She once told me firmly, "Don't feel sorry for me." We didn't, we were just inspired. That's her legacy.'

PETER SISSONS

'The first time I met Buckit I thought she had a certain sparkle and she never lost it. She was the most wonderful friend and always showed more concern for others than for herself. I loved her sense of fun and humour, and I will always miss her laugh.'

SARAH BYRNE (Nutch) – Friend since College

'Helen is a great loss to sport. Her easy manner made her a natural for live broadcasting. But her enthusiasm for all sports and commitment to the involvement of young people in sport set her apart.'

KATE HOEY – Minister for Sport

'Helen was a generous colleague and friend. I'll miss her reassuring presence in the *Six o'Clock News* studio. She was a wonderful team player. It has been an honour to know and work with her.'

HUW EDWARDS

'Undoubtedly the greatest fighter I've ever worked with was Helen Rollason.'

FRANK DICK

'She broke new ground in TV and went on defying the odds to the end. We'll remember her as much for her courage as her professionalism and humour.'

JOHN MOTSON

'Through her unconditional friendship she gave one of the greatest gifts of all – the right to be myself.'

DEB CROOK – Friend from the age of eleven

'Thank you, Helen Rollason – you are an inspiration – thank you for everything. You're a bloody little marvel and I give you all my strength. You don't need my courage as you have more than ten men.'

Letter from a well-wisher, July 1999

Helen's Contribution to Cancer Awareness

Dr Neville Davidson, Consultant Oncologist and Chairman of the HEAL Cancer Charity

When I first met Helen Rollason in early September 1997, it was clear that I was dealing with a special person. Quite how special, I was to discover over the months – almost two years – that followed.

If there ever is such a thing as a model patient, then Helen would have to qualify for the title. She approached every discussion on her treatment with complete clarity and total honesty, asking probing questions about treatment options and participating fully in decisions. Nothing was hidden on either side, and once decisions were taken, she let it be known that the doctors and nurses enjoyed her complete trust.

Helen's courage and determination has been well recorded in newspaper tributes and the BBC programme *Hope for Helen*. From a medical point of view, I have no doubt that her determination was a vital factor in keeping her going much longer than might have been anticipated by the advanced stage her cancer had reached at the time of diagnosis. She knew exactly how ill she was, and many people would have given up in the face of that knowledge. But not Helen – there was no way that she was going to admit defeat. She set about her battle against the disease with courage and tenacity, always looking ahead and setting goals and targets. With each goal achieved, she would look for the next. When setbacks occurred, she showed that she could weather them and return with determination undiminished. If one drug didn't work then she would be immediately ready to try the next one, never deterred by fears of possible side effects.

It goes without saying that Helen was an inspiration to other cancer sufferers. Many patients have told me how valuable her example was to them. But she also illustrated an important point about cancer treatment and normal life. There is a commonly held view that the increased longevity offered by chemotherapy may be outweighed by the attendant suffering and discomfort. Helen showed that to be false. She demonstrated that it was possible to control the cancer, to maintain a reasonable quality of life, to work and to accomplish so much, in spite of continuous treatment – more than fifty chemotherapy sessions – over a period of twenty-one months.

My colleagues and I were delighted when Helen agreed to give her name to the appeal which aims to set up a new cancer care centre at North Middlesex Hospital. In fact she gave more than just her name. She played her full part in helping to determine the objectives of the Centre, in publicising it and in raising funds. She was particularly keen that the Centre should make a priority of improving early detection – a concern which arose from her own experience of late diagnosis – and this has been incorporated into our aims.

The Helen Rollason Cancer Care Centre Appeal will continue. Our hope and expectation is that, within the not too distant future, we will be able to turn this vision into a reality offering major benefits to patients, their friends and families. It will be a fitting memorial to a very special person.

Dr Neville Davidson FRCP FRCR

The Helen Rollason Cancer Care Centre

The Helen Rollason Centre will provide a five-step approach to cancer care.

1 Prevention and screening

2 Improved diagnosis and treatment

3 Leading edge research into new treatments

4 Holistic therapies in conjuncton with conventional medicine

5 An environment where parents, family and friends feel comfort and security

To make a donation, or for further information about fund-raising possibilities, please contact:

Helen Rollason Cancer Care Centre Appeal
Room 40, The Cancer Centre
The North Middlesex Hospital
Sterling Way
Edmonton
London N18 1QX
Telephone: 020 8887 2293
Fax: 020 8887 2408

Cheques should be made payable to: Helen Rollason Cancer Care Centre Appeal

Telephone donations (credit card or debit card) may be made on 020 8887 2293

The Helen Rollason Cancer Care Centre Appeal is a division of HEAL Cancer Charity. (Registered Charity No.1052861)

Photographic Acknowledgements

We would like to thank the following for permission to reproduce photographs:

AllSport, *The Bath Evening Chronicle*, BBC Television, Roger Buxton/Essex FM, John Exelby, *Express* Newspapers, The London Marathon, *Mirror* Syndication International, John Motson, News International Newspapers, *OK! Magazine*, PA News, Rex Features, Thames Television.

Special thanks to members of staff at BBC Television for their help in providing photographs.